Chronic Illness During Childhood and Adolescence

About the series . . .

Series Editor: Alan E. Kazdin, Western Psychiatric Institute

The Sage series in **Developmental Clinical Psychology and Psychiatry** is uniquely designed to serve several needs of the field. While the primary focus is on childhood psychopathology, the series also offers monographs prepared by experts in clinical child psychology, child psychiatry, child development, and related disciplines. The series draws upon multiple disciplines, as well as diverse views within a given discipline.

In this series . . .

Chronic Illness During Childhood and Adolescence

Psychological Aspects

**William T. Garrison
Susan McQuiston**

Volume 19
Developmental Clinical Psychology and Psychiatry

SAGE PUBLICATIONS
The Publishers of Professional Social Science
Newbury Park   London   New Delhi

For David and Sean

For information address:

SAGE Publications, Inc.
2111 West Hillcrest Drive
Newbury Park, California 91320

SAGE Publications Ltd.
28 Banner Street
London EC1Y 8QE
England

SAGE Publications India Pvt. Ltd.
M-32 Market
Greater Kailash I
New Delhi 110 048 India

Printed in the United States of America

Library of Congress Cataloging-in-Publication Data

Garrison, William T.

    Chronic illness during childhood and adolescence : psychological aspects / William T. Garrison and Susan McQuiston.
      p.   cm. — (Developmental clinical psychology and psychiatry series ; 19)
    Bibliography: p.
    Includes indexes.
    ISBN 0-8039-3332-0. — ISBN 0-8039-3333-9 (pbk.)
    1. Chronic diseases in children—Psychological aspects.
2. Chronic diseases in adolescence—Psychological aspects.
I. McQuiston, Susan. II. Title. III. Series: Developmental
clinical psychology and psychiatry series ; v. 19.
    [DNLM: 1. Chronic Disease—in adolescence. 2. Chronic Disease—in
infancy & childhood. 3. Chronic Disease—psychology. W1 DE997NC
v. 19 / WS 200 G242c]
RJ380.G37   1989
155.4—dc19
DNLM/DLC
for Library of Congress   89-5989
                                         CIP

FIRST PRINTING 1989

CONTENTS

SERIES EDITOR'S INTRODUCTION

Interest in child development and adjustment is by no means new. Yet, only recently has the study of children benefited from advances in both clinical and scientific research. Advances in the social and biological sciences, the emergence of disciplines and subdisciplines that focus exclusively on childhood and adolescence, and greater appreciation of the impact of such influences as the family, peers, and schools have helped accelerate research on developmental psychopathology. Apart from interest in the study of child development and adjustment for its own sake, the need to address clinical problems of adulthood naturally draws one to investigate precursors in childhood and adolescence.

Within a relatively brief period, the study of psychopathology among children and adolescents has proliferated considerably. Several different professional journals, annual book series, and handbooks devoted entirely to the study of children and adolescents and their adjustment document the proliferation of work in the field. Nevertheless, there is a paucity of resource material that presents information in an authoritative, systematic, and disseminable fashion. There is a need within the field to convey the latest developments and to represent different disciplines, approaches, and conceptual views to the topics of childhood and adolescent adjustment and maladjustment.

The Sage Series on *Developmental Clinical Psychology and Psychiatry* is designed to serve uniquely several needs of the field. The Series encompasses individual monographs prepared by experts in the fields of clinical child psychology, child psychiatry, child development, and related disciplines. The primary focus is on developmental psycopathology which refers broadly here to the diagnosis, assessment, treatment, and prevention of problems that arise in the period from infancy through adolescence. A working assumption of the Series is that understanding, identifying, and treating problems of youth must draw on multiple disciplines and diverse views within a given discipline.

The task of individual contributors is to present the latest theory and research on various topics including specific types of dysfunction, diagnostic and treatment approaches, and special problem areas that affect

7

adjustment. Core topics within clinical work are addressed by the Series. Authors are asked to bridge potential theory, research and clinical practice, and to outline the current status and future directions. The goals of the Series and the tasks presented to individual contributors are demanding. We have been extremely fortunate in recruiting leaders in the fields who have been able to translate their recognized scholarship and expertise into highly readable works on contemporary topics.

The present book, completed by Drs. William T. Garrison and Susan McQuiston, focuses on *Chronic Illness During Childhood and Adolescence: Psychological Aspects.* The book integrates research from several areas to address the scope of the problem of chronic illness and the impact on children and their families. Chronic illness encompasses a large number of disorders among children and adolescents. Many are discussed specifically in this book including cancers, heart diseases, Acquired Immunodeficiency Syndrome (AIDS) among pediatric populations, and others. The effects of chronic disease on the child are traced from infancy through adolescence and through diverse domains of psychological and social functioning. The impact of childhood disease on the parents, siblings, and family functioning are addressed as well. Thus, the book at once considers both a developmental and contextual focus to convey the multiple consequences that chronic disease presents. Theory, research, and clinical issues are woven unusually well to describe the prevalence of dysfunction, to chart the impact on development, and to illustrate the breadth of consequences on the family. Case studies make poignant the complex and urgent issues that management and treatment require. The authors have produced a thorough and thoughtful evaluation of the field.

—*Alan E. Kazdin, Ph.D.*

1

INTRODUCTION

From a humanistic perspective it can be argued that the moral status of a particular society or civilization can be determined, in some measure, by its willingness and ability to care for its less fortunate, disenfranchised, or impaired members. In a related and more pragmatic vein, the future potency of a nation relies strongly upon its capacity to nurture and promote the health and education of its children, who are the wellspring for both the maintenance and enhancement of any society. However, these noble aspirations have not necessarily extended to those who are deemed to be out of the mainstream of a competitive, productivity-oriented society such as the United States. For example, systems designed to meet the needs of the heterogeneous population of American children typically have not been as attentive to the special needs of subgroups, such as the chronically ill or physically handicapped child. It is our view that the care of the chronically ill child, and the family which provides the context for her development, has not been a major or even minor focus in organized health care or domestic policy in the United States during the past century.

One broad reason that may help to account for this state of affairs is the relatively recent elevation in the social and legal status of children in general. This process has been documented as beginning, in any formal sense, only during the early part of the twentieth century (Aries, 1962; de Mause, 1974; Zelizer, 1985). Also, the eradication of major infectious childhood diseases has been a relatively recent development. Dramatic strides in prevention of such dread diseases during this century have resulted in an increased interest in the numbers of chronically ill children seen within pediatric medical practice. It is likely that improved longevity in this group of children and adolescents will continue this trend. Pediatric medicine's burgeoning focus on a *new morbidity*, a term which refers to children and adolescents at risk by virtue of behavioral, social, and developmental factors (Haggerty, Roghmann, & Pless, 1975; Cohen, 1984), promises to reap benefits for the chronically ill child. This process has also just begun, however, and it remains to be seen how the emphasis on psychosocial and developmental issues in pediatric practice will eventually be implemented, given the limitations of existing health care systems and even resistance from within pediatric medicine's own ranks. In any event, it is likely that mental health related professionals will continue to be called upon to provide supportive and therapeutic contributions. Because of this fact, the topic of adjustment to childhood chronic illness and broader questions regarding individual and family coping with chronic life stress become pertinent to clinical practice and research.

ILLUSTRATIVE CASE VIGNETTES

We would like to initially present a number of case vignettes which serve to illustrate many of the issues involved in attempts to understand and assist chronically ill children and their families. These descriptions of children and families encountering chronic diseases or conditions, and the potential occurrence of psychological maladjustment, should set the stage for our subsequent review of research and clinical studies on the psychological aspects of illness during childhood and adolescence. It is our belief that many of the important issues revealed in the research and theoretical literature on this subject are dramatically played out within the narratives derived from individual case histories. We will intersperse references to critical questions in the professional and clinical literature between these vignettes to remind the reader that the stories of these children resonate with important concerns regarding the nature of psychosocial impairment in the chronically ill and the potential role of psychologically oriented clinicians who seek to provide assistance. It is equally important that we seek to communicate the role of key clinical concepts in our attempts to understand and help chronically ill children and their families. A review of the current empirical research literature can only bring the clinician so far, just as the quantitative data collected in empirical studies can fail to fully inform our theoretical attempts to explain the full range of individual variation.

Thomas

Spina bifida was diagnosed in Thomas at his birth. The child was born with *meningomyelocele* with a fibrous sac located on his malformed spinal cord filled with CNS fluid. Some neurologic deficits and partial paralysis were observed in the child's lower limbs and in the cutaneous areas surrounding the sac. No other gross physical abnormalities or perinatal complications were noted at that time. The primiparous (first child) mother was not allowed to hold or see the baby at delivery since the child was immediately sent to the hospital's intensive care unit to minimize the risk of infectious complications. The baby's parents were told of the diagnosis and given limited information about the situation by the attending obstetrician and a delivery room nurse who suggested that the pediatrician would be best qualified to provide the details.

Both mother and father reacted initially with a mixture of emotions, predominantly with fearfulness and anxiety. The initial visit with the pediatrician occurred the next morning during her regular nursery rounds. She attempted to answer their questions and inform the parents about the medical possibilities which might occur, especially the high likelihood for immediate surgical intervention and the potential neurological consequences, notably *hydrocephalus* which she described as a potentially dangerous increase in fluid pressure on their baby's brain. The pediatrician told the parents that the child would be sent immediately to the regional medical center and treated in the neonatal intensive care unit. She indicated that the neonatologists, pediatric neurologists, and surgeons there would be available to more fully discuss the decisions that needed to be made for the care of their new baby. At the medical center the family was assigned to a clinical team which included a medical social worker called in to support the parents and to help facilitate their learning and coping with the difficulties associated with this diagnosis.

Within a few days the parents were made familiar with an array of short- and long-term possibilities, including the uncertain future for the child in regard to eventual level of functioning and his overall quality of life. Psychological counseling was requested by the parents who were asked to decide whether or not to allow immediate surgery to close the sac. An array of potential consequences began to overwhelm both parents who felt unable to decide what to do. Initially two themes became evident in working with this family. First, the lack of information and attention to their emotional needs during the first few hours after the child's delivery led to problems later in communicating with medical staff about the care of the baby and in parental decision making. Prior to this point the parents had felt very much left out of the decisional process relevant to their baby and yet later perceived themselves as being given rather burdensome responsibilities for which they were unprepared and uninformed. Secondly, the mother displayed an intense emotional upset and ambivalence over being with the child, even when told she could hold the child briefly and with precaution (two days after delivery). The father showed less overt emotional upset but had not sought to hold the child throughout their ordeal. Mother articulated her upset in terms of both a fear of hurting the child and as deriving from the unanticipated shock of producing a "defective" child. To make the situation even more complicated, clinical intervention with the family was also being rushed due to the need for immediate and critical decisions regarding surgery and other medical procedures intended to maximize the infant's viability.

Commentary. At least three issues merit discussion in this case. First, the abrupt and potentially traumatic aspects associated with these parents learning their child was seriously ill may often characterize the initial diagnosis of a chronic childhood disease or condition. Further, the aftershocks of such a process can be felt even years later and manifest themselves in a host of ways including provider-patient relations, medical and psychosocial help-seeking, ongoing behavioral patterns in response to crisis, and so on. In this particular case the family became more and more suspicious of medical personnel and viewed the process as a rather cold and impersonal one which had left them feeling confused, isolated, and increasingly angry. Several studies examining initial reactions to traumatic events such as the birth of a deformed or seriously ill child, discovering your child has a chronic disease or handicapping condition, and other stressful life events, have combined to suggest that close attention should be paid to the coping mechanisms employed by parents and children immediately after such disrupting life occurrences. Also, the approaches of medical providers and/or clinical service teams need to be examined to determine which seem to promote better or worse initial adjustment and coping by the family and child. Consider the case of health education which typically takes place following a medical diagnosis. Too much information presented to children and families initially can often overwhelm them, especially if the psychoemotional impact has not been addressed or assuaged. Similarly, too little information or structure following diagnosis can also lead to more serious adjustment problems later in the course of the disease or treatment. The clinician is often left with difficult decisions concerning the adequate level of education or preparation, decisions which may affect eventual adjustment outcomes.

A second issue that emerges from this brief vignette is one that appears throughout much clinical work with the parents of chronically ill children, namely, the loss of an idealized child. This can result when the child's condition varies so greatly from what was thought to be normal and expectable in childrearing that the resulting parental sense is that the child is essentially imperfect or defective. This phenomenon can yield an array of responses in parents, siblings, and the extended families of such children, perhaps most pronounced and dramatic in the case of the newborn or infant. In this particular case the issue arose even before the parents had an opportunity to experience what it is like to have a normal child, let alone consider the arrival of a baby who may bring considerable financial, personal and psychological burdens into their lives. The emotions associated with this potential issue can run the gamut from intense anger to hopelessness and depression, feelings which are likely to fall within the normal range of psychological coping and should be considered appropriate human responses to serious trauma of this kind. It is a theme which can present itself in clinical work with families of the chronically ill child, and it is one that needs to be anticipated and explored delicately by the therapist, counselor or medical provider.

Another aspect of this case which bears noting is the sense of urgency associated with psychosocial consultations in health care settings. Many factors can precipitate this common situation. In brief, the clinician is often presented with situations that require rapid establishment of rapport, a grasp of complicated technical details of a particular case, and a need to facilitate and support difficult decisions by parents and patients. This scenario points out the immense value of including the principles of crisis intervention and management in the armamentarium of the professional who works with the chronically ill.

Mary Ellen

Mary Ellen was a 9-year-old child diagnosed with *acute lymphoblastic leukemia* (ALL) soon after a protracted period of flu-like symptoms including elevated fever, respiratory difficulties, loss of appetite, lack of energy, and persistent body pains. Her treating physician, a pediatric oncologist located forty miles from her home, recommended an initial hospital stay of three to four weeks to stabilize the child's condition and then a six to twelve month course of chemotherapy, which included use of several potent anti-cancer drugs. Her response to this regimen of chemotherapy over the course of the year would determine the need for other medical interventions. Since the child and family were judged to be coping fairly well with both the diagnosis and the prospects of the prescribed treatments, no psychosocial support was deemed necessary, although the parents were given the name of a local support group sponsored by the *American Cancer Society*. Indeed, the initial months following the start of chemotherapy were characterized by a general hopefulness and adoption of a positive attitude toward the disease by parents and child alike. The child soon returned to school and performed at a high level both academically and socially. She continued to be active in social and sport activities, although side effects from the medicine she was administered occasionally interfered with her ability to participate fully. The child did not lose much of her hair in the initial period following the start of chemotherapy, although she was warned this might occur at some point.

The child was referred to a pediatric psychologist later in the course of treatment when she failed to go into remission. This meant that her leukemia was not controlled and that additional chemotherapy protocols (the administration of anti-cancer drugs in combination over time) would need to be implemented. The observed impact of this news on the parents and child, along with the realization of a decreased survivability esti- mate, was judged to be major with both parents reporting rather sudden and significant deterioration in functioning and attitude, including an increase in marital discord. The parents described the experience as hitting the lowest point on a "rollercoaster ride," their own analogy for the cancer-related life event.

The child, for the first time following diagnosis, began to overtly express anger and frustration over the disease, its effect on her life and family, and the failure of the doctors to cure her. She became less compliant regarding visits to the physician and the need for occasional hospitalizations. Her school work and social relations suffered along with a diminishing physical status and a gradual decrease in optimism regarding the ultimate outcome. She began to talk about the likelihood of her own death and what that would be like, almost always accompa- nied by intense and uncontrollable emotionality, manifest predominantly in a fearful sadness. She displayed prolonged periods of crying and sadness both at home and in the hospital, which were clearly exacerbated by her current deteriorating physical condition and frequent bouts with the pain and inconvenience associated with ongoing medical tests and interventions.

   Commentary. There is some suggestion in the professional literature on cancer in children that the psychological response may be closely correlated with the ultimate length of the illness and the specific history of the child's response to various treatments along the way (Koocher and O'Malley, 1981; Van Dongen-Melman and Sanders-Woudstra, 1986). Short-term coping in most patients appears quite good after the initial shock and disappointment of such a major, life-threatening diagnosis. It appears in many cases that it is only as the course of the disease and its treatment wear on that more serious symptoms of psychological and familial stress will be perceived or manifested. And, as with adults affected by disease, the relationship between the child's current level of physical discomfort or pain caused by the cancer and the relatively potent treatments and the overall adequacy of psychological coping is a rather direct one. That is, the more pain there is to bear the harder it can be to adequately or successfully cope. Also, the more disappointments related to treatment failures, the greater the likelihood for negative effects from the disease. The cancer literature concerning both adults and children, however, serves to teach us about the immense psychological strength human beings appear to possess in times of intense and protracted stress. For most patients, the erosion of this strength in the face of increasing duress is an extremely understandable process, and not at all a psychopathological one. As the burdens increase, however, the need and value of psychosocial interventions become more apparent.

   This child's rather rapid decrease in functioning, partially brought about by deterioration in physical functioning, could also be attributed to a growing sense of hopelessness, generalized anger, and fear of the unknown, namely her own imminent demise. We may be better served by not prescribing a psychological treatment in such a case, but thinking and behaving as psychosocial resources for such children and their families. The term *supportive counseling* comes closest to capturing what must go on between a child such as Mary Ellen and her caretakers and loved ones. Seeking a curative that will somehow work independent of the many forces that reside outside our personal and professional control, namely the child's eventual response to medical intervention and the resulting course of her disease, is often a foolish quest. And yet, children with serious and life-threatening illnesses who also display psychological *symptoms* such as sadness, anger, anxiety, prolonged discontentment, and hopelessness are often referred to psychological

family in the face of chronic disease's immense burdens. Bobby's high level of functioning prior to the emergence of CF's debilitating and disfiguring features was largely due to the strength he derived from a family that remained continually supportive of and interpersonally connected to him. His maturity, noted by all who encountered him, was rooted in a familial coping style that allowed him to be special and normal at the same time.

In a related vein, the role of siblings in both the care of the chronically ill child *and* in buffering parents from the impact of life stress is illustrated in this case example. This is an area just beginning to receive deserved attention both in terms of other children in the affected families as *resources* to the affected child and parents, as well as the possible psychological effects upon the siblings themselves. It is likely that future clinical work with the chronically ill child and family will continue to explore and address this issue.

Bobby's acute sensitivity to hand and foot clubbing was again a reasonable psychological response to what would be an extremely upsetting physical change for a preadolescent or adolescent child. The new feelings Bobby described, although certainly precipitated in recent developments and the changing nature of his disease, may also have been derived from developmental changes in his ability to understand the full impact of CF on his life and longevity. Solutions for Bobby's situation do not come easily, of course, and "treatment" might again consist of supportive counseling, a sorting out of those feelings and thoughts which give rise to problems in functioning. Anxiety-reduction strategies might be useful to this boy, but only through a careful exploration of his current psychological coping and the changes that have precipitated his social withdrawal and emerging fear of death.

Christina

Christina was a 2 1/2-year-old child diagnosed, after several months of various physical symptoms, with insulin-dependent diabetes mellitus (IDDM). There was a history of IDDM in two cousins of the parents but no other immediate family member was reported to have the disease. Maternal grandmother lived nearby and was diagnosed with Type-2, non-insulin dependent diabetes which was associated with her advanced age. Christina was described by her mother as a healthy, happy, and well-behaved child until several months prior to the medical diagnosis. During that time she had noted an increased irritability in the child, and sporadic but rather dramatic increases in her frequency of urination (*polyuria*), intake of liquids (*polydipsia*), and overall appetite (*polyphagia*). Due to a fluctuation in both the occurrence and intensity of Christina's symptoms, her family physician was unable to diagnose a specific problem in the child for over two months, and the initial impression of a viral influenza seemed less and less plausible as the symptoms reappeared and continued. Once the diagnosis was finally made the parents and child were referred to a pediatric nurse practitioner for education about juvenile diabetes and the skills necessary for treating the disease.

Within a year of diagnosis Christina's mother reported that her ability to manage the child's behavior, and the overall quality of their relationship, had deteriorated considerably. Professional help was sought and the family was referred to a clinical psychologist. After an initial session with this local psychologist the parents were largely unsatisfied, reportedly due to the clinician's lack of technical knowledge about the disease itself. During the initial session they felt they were educating the psychologist about diabetes more than getting to the heart of the matter they wished to discuss. They then sought out a therapist with specific experience in the area of juvenile diabetes. Eventually they were referred to another psychologist whose office was 25 miles from their own community but decided to make an appointment since they felt the child's behavioral problems were worsening.

The initial sessions revealed intense struggles around blood glucose monitoring, dietary changes, and insulin injections which now interfered with the mother's previous relations with Christina. Soon after diagnosis the mother had decided that she would assume responsibility for the tasks required to monitor the child's disease, taking it upon herself to impose a regular schedule for testing and injections, making changes in the child's diet accordingly, and ensuring that the child engaged in adequate amounts of physical exercise. She described a daily battle with her child over these tasks. Over time she felt Christina had developed an oppositional stance to her disease regimen which, in turn, appeared to affect her compliance with other requests of the parents. The child was assessed to manifest behaviors somewhat typical of the normal 3 1/2-year-old with the exception of elevated parent-child discord and a tendency to display increased irritability associated with periods when she was found to be in relatively poor metabolic control of her diabetes. This latter fact seemed to be more true in recent months than in the period immediately following diagnosis when she was consistently in good metabolic control. In fact, during the time after diagnosis a "honeymoon period" had occurred in which the child's disease seemed controlled largely independent of her regimen adherence, a fact which led to problems later on.

The therapist explored several key issues with the parents: First, the father's relative absence from the day-to-day management of the child; secondly, the possibility of including the child in some way in the treatment regimen for her own disease, which had not been attempted as yet; and thirdly, the manner in which the disease diagnosis had altered the parental views of the child, their responses to her, and the child's resulting perceptions about the disease and changes in parenting style.

Commentary. Again we would like to highlight two important issues common in clinical work with chronically ill children and their parents. There is a critical need for clinicians to attempt to familiarize themselves with, and understand the ways in which the features and onset of a particular disease entity can impact, shape, and alter normal child and family development. Christina's oppositional behavior, perhaps exacerbated by the onset of her diabetes as is suggested in the case description, originated within rather typical and predictable phases common to the preschool period involving more frequent power struggles and an intensification of conflict between parent and child. These phenomena are hypothesized to derive from the child's expression of strivings for increased autonomy and a more active resistance to disliked activities such as cleaning up one's own messes, getting to dinner on time or sitting still for prolonged periods, and other assorted parent-generated expectations which may not fit well with child capacities. This process can also expectedly characterize the relatively noxious activities associated with the diabetes treatment regimen, which can include frequent fingerpricks, injections, and lifestyle modifications which the child views as substantial. Thus, increased oppositionality in this child can be accounted for through a rather reasonable process, the exploration and understanding of which can often be quite helpful to the frustrated and bewildered parent.

A second issue illustrated in this case involves the appropriate role of the affected child, mother and/or father, and the child's siblings in the care of a chronic disease or condition. Typically, it is the mother who is most intimately and routinely involved with performing many of the required activities associated with her child's chronic illness. It is rather common in clinical cases to encounter families in which the father plays a relatively minor role in this area other than to reinforce the mother's requests to the child or to serve as a substitute caretaker who knows little about the disease and its regimen. Also illustrated in this case is the common issue concerning when and how much a child should engage in self-care skills for their own disease. Some controversy over this issue has been seen in the professional literature with some writers suggesting that this begin at very early ages, while others have warned that it should be attempted after certain cognitive and motivational milestones have been achieved. Most researchers and clinicians recommend assigning the child responsibilities for self-care commensurate with reasonable expectations based on a judgment about the child's current cognitive, behavioral and motivational status. Given that these criteria are met, most writers have suggested the child should be *actively* and *optimally* involved in their own care. Despite this rational view, some parents and health care practitioners alike will behave more in the extreme, for example, by effectively rendering the child as a largely passive recipient of medical and lifestyle-related procedures until much later in the childhood period. And, conversely, some parents may give children too much responsibility in their own health care, in part due to their own psychological issues related to the disease or as a result of more generalized problems in the family which affect behavioral compliance, attention to disease-related tasks, or organization of the regimen.

John

John was a 15-year-old diagnosed with *hemophilia* at the age of three who was referred for psychological assistance several months after testing positively for *Human Immunodeficiency Viral Syndrome* (HIV). Although John was currently asymptomatic, a positive HIV test carries with it the same level of infectious risk as a case of full-blown AIDS. Because of this fact, John and his parents felt that even minimal infectious risk made it necessary to inform John's school officials of the situation so that necessary precautions could be taken to inform and protect other children. Considerable effort was made to ensure that overreaction by children and their parents did not occur, and the likelihood of this was reduced by the fact that the school had previously enrolled another child with the diagnosis of AIDS and subsequent educational activities had taken place. That child had continued in school until several months prior to his death due to complications of the disease. Now, however, a different set of teachers, not involved with the previous child, needed to be informed and assisted with planning for normalizing John's school situation as much as possible. Despite the previous experience with AIDS in John's school and community, and the largely humane treatment he received by his peers and teachers, several stressful occurrences disrupted this situation. A noticeable decrease in school attendance in John's classes, a few threatening phone calls to his home, and subtle but significant alterations in his relations with peers and teachers were reported. Indeed, John often found himself without anyone to be with after school, where previously he had been a rather popular young man. This situation led to acute feelings of alienation and anger over his situation, where prior to this he had been reported to cope very well with his hemophilia and the required treatments. Also, John understood very well the ramifications of the positive HIV diagnosis and the resulting uncertainty about his future filled his thoughts.

Commentary. It is important to note that John's parents' decision to inform his school officials and other members of his and their community was, at that time, completely voluntary. At the time of this writing, a positive HIV laboratory test remains confidential information even among those health care providers who will be encountering the patient in the future. This situation may change as the sheer numbers of AIDS-affected patients increase, but the current level of social stigma associated with this infectious disease apparently overshadows the fear of mass contagion in the general population. In this case, unlike other very real cases related to AIDS infection, the overall response to the child's situation was essentially well thought out and quite positive. However, John's exposure to the virus led to subtle yet psychologically disturbing problems.

This rather extreme case, although it is becoming more common with passing time, illustrates the possible psychological and social consequences of a chronic illness or condition about which the vast majority of the lay public will often know very little. This situation is rapidly changing in the case of AIDS, however, since the government and media have increased educational intervention. In John's case the changes in peer relations and general perception of his place in his own world (e.g., school) led to emotional difficulties and very real social isolation. A therapeutic approach to these thoughts and feelings, as well as the harsh realities of his positive testing, will need to evolve along with changing attitudes about the risk AIDS poses to the general population. We are only at the beginning of this process which promises to remain a major health care issue during the coming years.

THE GOALS OF THE BOOK

At this juncture, we should specify the goals and major themes which helped to guide the creation of this book. Our initial task was to inform the reader about the most prevalent and clinically relevant types of chronic illness which can affect children and youth, with special attention to the features of illness which are pertinent to child psychological development and the course of family relations.

Our second goal was to selectively review the empirical literature on psychosocial and developmental aspects of chronic childhood illness in a manner which would be clinically useful. That is, our review seeks to inform the clinical and educational process whereby these children will eventually derive their medical, psychological and familial treatment and support. We have attempted to pay close attention to apparent *disease-specific* findings versus *disease-global* findings, that is, results which seem to apply only to certain disease entities versus those which have broader application across diseases. And, our review is intended to reflect upon three major themes which characterize our view on chronic childhood illness, described below.

The research literature and clinical work with chronically ill children and their families have been largely based upon either *pathology or personality* models, or in other words, on how and when things go awry. Our review shares this focus at times, and we would argue it is a legitimate perspective in some cases since there is evidence to support the position that such children appear to manifest higher rates of psychological symptomatology and are at elevated risk for psychological and psychiatric dysfunction as compared to heterogeneous groups of non-affected children (Haggerty, 1984; Breslau, 1985; Drotar & Bush, 1985; Pless, 1984). However, a major goal of our discussion is to highlight and illustrate the fact that adjustment to chronic illness in children and their families more often provides a context for understanding psychological health and successful adaptation, both in the child and in the family. Because of this, models of psychopathology or personality aberration are often inappropriate and fall short of accurately characterizing the process of adjustment to chronic disease. *Psychological coping, degree of functional impairment,* and *quality of life* are terms we return to again and again as typically providing a more appropriate and useful clinical and research vocabulary compared with constructs such as *pathology, psychiatric symptomatology,* or *disorder.* We also argue that such an approach to understanding chronic illness and psychological sequelae allows a greater opportunity to study psychological strength, resilience, and resistance to life stress.

A second major theme in this book involves the usefulness of applying a developmental perspective to the child and family affected by a chronic illness. The research literature on normal and atypical child populations is helpful to us in sketching out a developmental framework for appreciating differences in the cognitive understanding of illness at various periods in childhood, the impact on social relationships, and its relevance to the course of parent-child relations. Fewer theories and studies exist, however, that will help us to understand equally important associations among the individual child's subjective understanding of illness, the behavioral and emotional sequelae of disease, and possible longer term effects on constructs such as the sense of self, emotional expression and development, and the emergent personality. Since we seek to emphasize the notion that chronic illness in childhood can teach us about psychological health and resilience, it is our task to demonstrate that developmental theories of cognition, self-perception, and emotion are necessary to comprehend the full range of the phenomenon.

Furthermore, the larger issues of child development, which empirical studies and child psychological theories provide, offer a useful backdrop for our discussion of how illness impacts on normal patterns of individual evolution and family interactions to create both stress and protection for the child. Thus, our third major theme revolves around the essential importance and role of the family in explaining and predicting eventual adjustment to chronic illness in childhood. Family and child will be seen as often inextricably combined and, therefore, our understanding of psychological coping with chronic disease will need to be appropriately attuned to this fact. Of course, many of the studies we consider have been extremely mindful of this and include attention to family factors and outcomes. This is one bias we gladly share with the modest empirical and clinical literature on psychological aspects of childhood chronic illness since it emphasizes an influence with both theoretical and clinical significance which cannot be denied.

Chapter 2 provides an overview of childhood disease that includes historical and contemporary perspectives on mortality and morbidity. This chapter also describes the epidemiology, features, and course of major childhood diseases. This basic background in the chronic diseases of childhood is intended to provide the reader with both factual information concerning childhood diseases and to impart a sense of the clinical issues found within this special population of children. We also hope to offer some insight into the psychological and developmental ramifications attendant to these disease entities when they occur during childhood and adolescence.

Chapter 3 more closely reviews and considers the theoretical and empirical literature dealing with developmental aspects of chronic illness onset and course in the child. This literature is not only theoretically interesting but it also contains a wealth of valuable clinical information particularly relevant to chronic illness during childhood.

Chapter 4 examines those studies that have attempted to measure the psychological and familial correlates and outcomes associated with chronic diseases in childhood and adolescence. Although we have already hinted at our overall orientation to a strict pathology view, it is important to review these studies as they relate to clinical decision making. Also, we hope that our discussion will highlight the strengths and weaknesses of previous research in this area.

Chapter 5 presents an overview of several major treatment approaches that are found in clinical practice and clinical outcome studies dealing with chronic illness during childhood and adolescence. We also consider the role various health-related professions have historically played in the delivery of psychosocial services to chronically ill children and their families.

Chapter 6 provides a brief overview of some of the major issues raised in this book. It also seeks to provide some guidance concerning new directions in research, clinical, and policy efforts.

2

OVERVIEW

HISTORICAL VIEW OF
CHILDHOOD MORTALITY AND MORBIDITY

Several historians of the childhood period have argued that it is the improved survivorship of children during the past few centuries, due largely to breakthroughs in medical technology, improved nutritional status, and the contribution of epidemiological investigations of childhood infectious disease, which has led to an enhancement of the child's economic and social value. However, it is likely that mortality rates during childhood have not been as constant across time nor as exceedingly high as some historians originally speculated. McLaughlin (1974) has pointed out that accurate estimates of childhood mortality are difficult to come by for the ninth through thirteenth century, although there is evidence these rates were substantially higher than in later centuries. Based upon historical and demographic documents, she estimates mortality during infancy to have been as high as two in three babies. A rate closer to one in three would die during the childhood period. Presumedly high mortality rates during the Middle Ages led to the view that children's highly unpredictable longevity contributed to a diminished emotional investment in children on the part of parents and the society-at-large. This remains a point of controversy, however.

Pollock (1987) summarizes historical data on childhood mortality during the period between the sixteenth and nineteenth centuries:

> From 1600 to 1900, the mortality rate for children under the age of one varied between 13 and 15 percent and was at its highest in the nineteenth century. The death rate for children aged up to nine varied between 22 and 28 percent, peaking in the nineteenth century. (p. 94)

She notes that one out of four children born during this period would die by the age of 9 years. However, her scholarly investigations of the personal memoirs and diaries of parents during the sixteenth through nineteenth century indicate that parents very probably focused more on the relative likelihood that their children would survive than on the possibility of unavoidable death, as other authors have suggested. This view has been criticized by historians who argue parents evidenced very limited emotional investment in their children until the mid to latter part of the nineteenth century (Stone, 1977; Pinchbeck & Hewitt, 1969; Badinter, 1981). Such critics also point out that the writings of the more highly educated and literary, who tended to come from the upper social classes of each era, offer decidedly skewed observations.

The diseases of childhood during the seventeenth century have been described as "worms, fevers of various sorts, smallpox, diphtheria, whooping cough, rickets and measles" (Pollock, 1987, p .93). During the eighteenth century "smallpox and rickets were at their height, and in the nineteenth century tuberculosis, diphtheria, and typhus were on the increase and cholera made its first appearance" (Pollock, 1987, p. 93). With the gradual introduction of inoculation procedures, and the slow but eventual acceptance of this practice by parents, the incidence of diseases such as smallpox was greatly reduced. Subsequently, tuberculosis reached high levels in childhood and adolescence from the latter part of the eighteenth through the early part of the twentieth century, until a vaccine was produced in 1921.

We would like to make two additional points based on our historical review. First, there is evidence to support the view that many parents strove to succor the ill or dying child and demonstrated considerable emotional upset in response to both the child's physical suffering and loss by death, regardless of the actual mortality or morbidity rates of the times. Secondly, despite evidence of this strong parental attachment to the ill child, few formal systems existed to ensure the provision of medical care. This was due to a lack of equal status for children under the law *and* a medical profession with little to offer by way of cures for deadly childhood diseases. Although primarily available to the higher social classes, we should note that some attention was paid to developing organized treatment facilities for children during the seventeenth through nineteenth centuries. These were primarily in the form of *sanitariums* which mixed adult and child patients and typically employed identical treatment procedures for both mental and physical disorders.

CONTEMPORARY PATTERNS OF CHRONIC ILLNESS

As noted previously, the focus of pediatric medicine in the United States has changed considerably during the past two centuries. As child survivability in Western nations has increased, and life-threatening illnesses have been better controlled through pharmacological innovation, we have witnessed a movement away from almost exclusive concerns about acute, infectious diseases to a more mixed focus on the remediation of common transient ailments of childhood, accidents and trauma, well-child care, developmental and behavioral guidance, and the ongoing care of the chronically ill or handicapped child. Table 2.1 displays the estimated incidence rates for various childhood marker diseases in the United States, the most chronic and prevalent of which will be the subject of our review.

Estimates of the total incidence of children with chronic illnesses and conditions range from 10% to about 12% in the general U.S. population with variation due to differences in survey methods (e.g., definitions and measures), sample location and characteristics, and timing of studies (Hobbs et al., 1985). This translates roughly to about 7.5 million children and adolescents. The majority of these children, about 75% to 80%, are presumed to be mildly to moderately affected by chronic illnesses and conditions (Haggerty, 1984), although psychosocial correlates and outcomes in this group are not well known. If we use overall impairment of functional status as an index of severity, (i.e., how seriously they are affected in terms of physical and intellectual limitations), the figure for children with major impacts from chronic illness and conditions is closer to 2% to 3% of the general population (Newacheck, Budetti & Halfon, 1986), or about 20% to 25% of all chronically ill children.

Figure 2.1 graphically displays the prevalence of activity limiting conditions during childhood and adolescence estimated between 1960 and 1982. More recent statistics covering the period 1983 to 1985 have essentially corroborated these earlier estimates, suggesting relative stability in prevalence for most chronic diseases and/or conditions (Collins, 1988).

Haggerty (1984) has specified that as many as one million children and adolescents in the United States have a severe chronic illness which merits ongoing, comprehensive medical care. He goes on to point out an additional ten million children with less serious chronic conditions who may be in need of regular monitoring and perhaps specialized care. He

TABLE 2.1

Estimated Prevalence of Chronic Diseases and Conditions in Children,
Ages 0-20 in the United States - 1980

Disorder	Prevalence Estimates Per 1000	Range of Prevalence Estimates Per 1000
Arthritis	2.2	1.0 - 3.0
Asthma	38.0	20.0 - 53.0
moderate to severe	10.0	8.0 - 15.0
Autism	.44	.40 - .48
Central nervous system injury		
traumatic brain injury	.05	—
paralysis	2.1	2.0 - 2.3
Cerebral palsy	2.5	1.4 - 5.1
Chronic renal failure	.080	—
terminal	.010	—
nonterminal	.070	—
Cleft lip/palate	1.5	1.3 - 2.0
Congenital heart disease	7.0	2.0 - 7.0
severe congenital heart disease	.50	
Cystic fibrosis	.20	—
Diabetes mellitus	1.8	1.2 - 2.0
Down syndrome	1.1	
Hearing impairment	16.	
deafness	.1	.06 - .15
Hemophilia	.15	
Leukemia		
acute lymphocytic leukemia	.11	
Mental retardation	25.0	20.0 - 30.0
Muscular dystrophy	.06	
Neural tube defect	.45	
spina bifida	.40	
encephalocele	.05	
Phenylketonuria	.10	
Sickle cell disease	.46	
sickle cell anemia	.28	
Seizure disorder	3.5	2.6 - 4.6
Visual impairment	30.0	20.0 - 35.0
impaired visual acuity	20.0	—
blind	.6	.5 - 1.0

SOURCE: Gortmaker, S. L., & Sappenfield, W. (1984). Chronic childhood disorders: Prevalence and impact. *Pediatric Clinics of North America*, *31*(1), 3-18. Used by permission of W. B. Saunders.

states that "most pediatricians in practice will care for 200 to 300 such children" (p. 1). Table 2.2 displays the breakdown by patient type in several primary care settings. As you will note, the chronically ill child

ACTIVITY LIMITATIONS AMONG CHILDREN

CASES PER 100,000

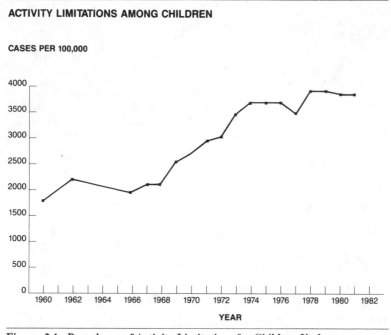

Figure 2.1 Prevalence of Activity Limitations for Children Under
17 Years of Age
SOURCE: Newacheck et al. (1986). Reprinted with permission.

accounts for about 10% to 14% of care given in the primary care setting
and somewhat less in family and general practices. Some more recent
estimates suggest this proportion may be growing (Johnson, 1988).
Pediatric subspecialists now attend to the medical needs of these children
as well, due to increased complexity and sophistication in both our
knowledge and treatment technologies for such illnesses. It is estimated
that approximately one-third of chronically ill children receive all of
their medical care from subspecialists only (Stein et al., 1983; Pless,
Satterwhite, VanVechten, 1978), with less than 20% receiving care in
both primary care and subspecialty settings (Perrin & Ireys, 1984).
However, most children with chronic illnesses receive regular medical
care in the primary pediatric or general practice setting. But, some
studies have suggested that up to one-third of chronically ill children do
not receive regular medical care at either primary or subspecialty levels
and less than 20% receive any social or mental health services (Walker,
Gortmaker & Weitzman, 1981; Cadman et al., 1986).

Table 2.2
Percent Distribution of Office Visits by Reason for Visit,
According to Physician Specialty; Children Less Than 15, United States, 1980*

MAJOR REASON FOR VISIT	ALL PHYSICIANS (N=7,658)	GENERAL OR FAMILY PRACTICE (N=1,628)	PEDIATRICS (N=4,408)	ALL SURGICAL (N=1,222)	INTERNAL MEDICINE (N=168)	OTHER MEDICAL SPECIALTIES (N=242)
Acute problem	51%	63%	53%	23%	51%	29%
Nonillness care	25	23	32	12	16	0
Chronic problem, routine	13	6	9	26	27	50
Chronic problem, flare-up	5	4	4	8	5	16
Postsurgery or postinjury	6	4	2	30	2	4

SOURCE: Gortmaker, S. L., & Sappenfield, W. (1984). Chronic childhood disorders: Prevalence and impact. *Pediatric Clinics of North America, 31*(1), 3-18. Used by permission of W. B. Saunders.

*Unpublished tabulations from the 1980 National Ambulatory Medical Care Survey, National Center for Health Statistics.

More specific analysis of health care service delivery systems and patient utilization relevant to chronic illnesses in children is revealing. For example, it has been reported that families with chronically ill children typically do not receive comprehensive psychosocial support within traditional medical settings despite a general awareness and acceptance of its potential importance in such cases (Stein et al., 1983). Less prevalent or lesser known disorders often do not have any specialized services available and parents are left to their own resources to construct a health care system which attempts to meet their child's needs. Also, while chronically ill children do receive a disproportionately greater amount of special education services in the United States and Canada, actual numbers of children in need of such services may be minimized through exclusion from public or private school systems that do not view acute or chronic illness as a legitimate special education category. For example, children with low school attendance due to recurrent symptomatology related to their chronic illness may not receive additional educational services (i.e., tutoring, modified teaching techniques, and so on), and may "fall between the cracks" in both school and health care systems. Pless and Roghmann (1971) highlighted the need for an array of disease-specific and disease-generic health care service delivery systems over 15 years ago. Progress in this area has been extremely slow, especially in rural and impoverished areas, inner-city locations, and with those diseases that have smaller prevalence rates or which require highly specialized medical care (Hobbs et al., 1985). This process has been hindered in general by lags in developing suitable reimbursement schemes, deficiencies in professional training, and ongoing problems with identifying those providers and health care systems that are best equipped and most predisposed to address these issues.

Mortality and Morbidity

The impact of disease on the mortality rates of children has stabilized during the past 30 years. The efforts of medical science and clinical practice have led to greater longevity for many children afflicted with more serious chronic diseases such as cystic fibrosis, diabetes mellitus, renal disease, cancer, and others. Hobbs et al. (1985) summarize the changing contribution of chronic illness to childhood mortality during this past century:

Congenital abnormalities contributed only 6.4 percent of infant deaths in 1915, but they now contribute 17.3 percent. Furthermore, in 1976 the death rate for congenitally malformed infants was about 40 percent of the 1915 rate; however, the rate for those without congenital malformations had declined to 13 percent of the 1915 rate. Actual deaths from chronic illnesses have declined moderately during the past few decades; the greatest improvement is in infectious diseases, which have been largely replaced by accidents, homicide, and suicide. (p. 37)

Table 2.3 depicts the expected mortality rates and concomitant longevity predictions for various classes of chronically ill children and adolescents in the United States.

The impact of chronic diseases on child and adult morbidity (the range of physical and functional consequences of an illness) is a more prevalent problem than mortality, at least in the United States and Western countries. Variation in morbidity patterns across disease groups is influenced by the range of severity of the particular disease, the specific organs or physical capacities which are affected, and a host of factors characterizing the individual case. And, as we noted earlier, various epidemiological surveys have suggested that from 1% to 3% of the child population have serious impairment due to a chronic illness or condition, with the observed variation again largely due to methods of measurement, the timing of surveys, and a gradual increase in longevity within the chronically ill subpopulation.

PSYCHOSOCIAL CORRELATES AND OUTCOMES

A broad range of psychosocial correlates and presumed outcomes of childhood chronic illness has been noted in various surveys and clinical reports. As one might predict, the severity of disease and its concomitant impact on the child's level of functioning tend to be consistently reported as mediating the likelihood for unmanageable stress and subsequent psychological sequelae. However, it is apparent that severity of disease and functional status alone do not account for the considerable variation that has been observed across disease types or even individual children with the same disease or condition (Steinhausen, Schindler, & Stephan, 1983; Daniels, Moos, Billings & Miller, 1987). As we noted previously, *brain-related* illnesses during childhood have been related to poorer psychologic and social outcomes as compared to non-brain-related disorders (Rutter et al., 1970; Breslau, 1985). And, *physical incapacitation* has been linked with higher risk likelihoods for psychiatric sequelae in children and adolescents (Drotar & Bush, 1985; Pless, 1984). Among the array of psychosocial correlates and outcomes mentioned in the profes-

TABLE 2.3

Prevalence and Survivability Estimates for
Eleven Childhood Chronic Diseases, Ages Birth to 20 Years,
United States, 1980

Disease	Estimated Proportion Surviving to Age 20* (percentage)	1980 Prevalence Estimate per 1,000**	Estimated Maximum Prevalence, Assuming 100% Survival to Age 20***
Asthma (moderate and severe)	98	10.00	10.20
Congenital heart disease	65	7.00	9.33
Diabetes mellitus	95	1.80	1.89
Cleft lip/palate	92	1.50	1.62
Spina bifida	50	.40	.67
Sickle cell anemia	90	.28	.29
Cystic fibrosis	60****	.20	.26
Hemophilia	90	.15	.16
Acute lymphocytic leukemia	40	.11	.22
Chronic renal failure	25	.08	.19
Muscular dystrophy	25	.06	.14
Estimated Total (assuming no overlap)		21.58	24.97

SOURCE: Gortmaker, S. L., & Sappenfield, W. (1984). Chronic childhood disorders: Prevalence
and impact. *Pediatric Clinics of North America*, *31*(1), 3-18. Used by permission of W. B. Saunders.
NOTE: *Estimate refers to the survival expected of a birth cohort to age 20, given current treatments.
        **Estimates are from population prevalence data or are derived from estimates of incidence
          (or prevalence at birth) and survival data.
      ***Most of the rates used in our calculations are not true incidence rates; rather, they are
          prevalence estimates at birth.
    ****1987 estimates would be over 80% of cases.

sional literature, family functioning and capacity to cope, overall levels
of life stress, the presence of additional chronic conditions, preexisting
personological characteristics of the child and parents, and
sociodemographic variables have all been suggested as mediators of the
relationship between chronic illness and psychiatric disorder. More
specifically, the list of individual psychosocial or developmental correlates and outcomes of chronic disease in children and adolescents includes presumed effects on overt behavior, the range and expression of
emotionality, alterations in self-perception and self-esteem, impaired
school performance and intellectual ability, effects on motivation and
personality, greater social isolation or feelings of alienation, and significant alterations in normal parent-child and sibling-child relationships.

Specific hypotheses about the effects of chronic illness on families and subsequent psychological outcomes have implicated various qualitative characteristics of family systems such as those dimensions of family environments proposed by Moos (1984), familial coping style and adaptational processes (Shapiro, 1983), and an array of sociodemographic factors such as poverty level, household composition, and marital status (Stein & Jessop, 1984; Cadman et al., 1986, 1987; Haggerty, Roghmann, & Pless, 1975). We shall review this literature in greater detail in Chapter 4 of this volume. However, it is important to highlight some issues relevant to the question of psychological and family outcomes deriving from chronic illness prior to a description of major childhood diseases.

First of all, the assumption that psychological or psychiatric disorder is common among those persons affected by chronic illness has been called into question both in the adult and child health research literatures (Cassileth, et al., 1984; Drotar, et al., 1981; Pless & Zvagulis, 1981). It is clear that a simple or direct relationship between chronic illness and psychosocial functioning does not exist. Rather, a wide range of responses to this source of life stress is more typical. While there is a good amount of evidence to suggest that depressive and anxiety-related symptomatology can be observed at higher rates in chronically ill adults (Kashani, Barbero, & Bolander, 1981), the effects on children are less clear. Several studies have reported elevated risk likelihoods for samples of chronically ill children, as compared with nonaffected children, for child and family psychological upset and diagnosable psychiatric disorders (Stein & Jessop, 1984a; Breslau, 1985; Cadman et al., 1987; Shapiro, 1983; Bedell, Giordani, Amour, Tavormina, & Bell, 1977; Pless, Roghmann & Haggerty, 1972). However, the estimates of the increase in risk likelihood range from a doubling of the rate observed in the physically well population to a more than ten-fold increase, again depending upon the particular measures and sampling techniques used in various studies. More conservative research suggests a two- to four-fold increase in risk for psychiatric disorder of some kind occurring at some point during the childhood and adolescent periods. This increase does not translate, however, into an adequate ability to predict outcomes for the individual case. And, by and large, few studies have offered longitudinal data that might shed light on the longer-term significance of chronic disease onset during childhood or adolescence.

Because of conflicting findings, several researchers have suggested broad-based interventions be used with this group of children and families until more specific models of negative outcome can be formulated and tested (Moos, 1984). And, as is typical of such controversial topics, at least one major study of adults with several types of chronic disease has implied that psychosocial interventions should not be population-wide since the actual rates of psychological or psychiatric dysfunction are uniformly low across major disease categories (Cassileth et al., 1984). With this view one would intervene only after significant problems arose, well after disease onset and after normal psychological coping processes have had sufficient time to evolve. One suspects that this may be the prevailing attitude of many primary-care providers currently in practice, given the rather low referral rates for chronically ill children to social and mental health subspecialists (Starfield & Borkowf, 1969; Gould, et al., 1980; Costello, 1988).

Those familiar with etiologic models of psychopathological conditions in childhood and adulthood, as well as the derivative recommendations for mental health prevention and intervention policies, will recognize the similarities between models of adaptation to chronic illness found in the child health literature (Johnson, 1986) and models of coping with other sources of life stress and trauma which seek to explain psychopathology. The role of biological predispositions has less prominence in models of poor-versus-good adjustment to chronic illness but it is likely that preexisting psychological capacities could be linked to biologic substrata in much the same way as they have been within psychiatric models. Indeed, the view that predisposition to mental disorder also serves to make the chronically ill child vulnerable to psychiatric dysfunction is apparent in the writings of influential child-psychiatric researchers in this area (Rutter, 1980). What is rather evident in the modest empirical and theoretical literature on psychosocial correlates and the sequelae of chronic disease in children is the rapidity and apparent ease with which numerous researchers and clinicians have imposed the etiologic and explanatory models of developmental psychopathology, as inadequate as they may be, on the case of chronically ill children. This certainly derives somewhat from the adult literature on chronic illness which was strongly influenced by the psychiatric models of stress, coping, and disorder, but it is also probably due to a marked absence of both theoretical and basic descriptive research attuned to the special characteristics and life context of the chronically ill. To reiterate an earlier point, emerging evidence suggests that reliance on a pathology model in the interpretation of the child and family response to chronic illness, while somewhat convenient, is inadequate in the majority of cases encountered in the medical setting.

MAJOR CHILDHOOD DISEASES

In this section we will briefly describe the more common childhood disease categories that provide the foundation for discussion in subsequent chapters. We have included *Pediatric Acquired Immunodeficiency Syndrome* (AIDS) which is reported to be on the rise in the United States, primarily because of the rather timely and unique aspects of this emerging disease. In subsequent chapters mention will be made of less prevalent diseases and/or conditions but only in the context of making a specific point.

In the remainder of this chapter we seek to provide basic information concerning disease *point prevalence* (the rate of the disorder in the population), the *incidence* (the rate of disorder during a specified period of time) and the *natural history* (etiology, clinical presentation and features, and course) of the disease during childhood and adolescence. We will also briefly consider suspected and documented developmental and psychosocial correlates for each disease. For a more extensive treatment of childhood disease categories the reader is directed to an excellent compendium contained in Hobbs, Perrin, and Ireys's book entitled *Chronic Illness in Childhood* (1985). We have gone to more recent clinical and review articles that contain updated and specific information concerning various diseases to make this overview more contemporary where possible. We believe strongly that such an overview is necessary to prepare the reader for the more detailed discussion of the behavioral and psychiatric research and clinical literature on various chronic illnesses as they relate to psychosocial and developmental issues. Also, knowledge about specific diseases of childhood will help to prepare the practitioner for a consideration of the range of possible approaches to clinical intervention with this special child population.

We should point out that definitions of chronic illness vary considerably, with some writers employing more traditional medical disease categories and others arguing that any *medical condition* that persists beyond a few months, and is severe in that it incapacitates or significantly impairs the child, should be included (Hobbs et al., 1985). We agree that researchers and clinicians interested in the psychosocial and developmental aspects of chronic illness should not exclude this latter group of children who present with more severe cases of various physical symptomatology since the outcomes in terms of impairment of function and psychologic adjustment can be quite similar. However, due to space considerations, we have chosen to focus primarily on chronic disease categories studied and reported in the more recent pediatric medicine and child health psychology literature since this provides a more specific and limited basis for our empirical review. Additionally, childhood handicapping conditions such as blindness, hearing impairment, posttraumatic sequelae, cerebral palsy, cranio-facial abnormalities, and autism are chronic conditions which require more exclusive attention than we are able to provide in this volume. However, we admit readily that such a demarcation of various chronic conditions and disease types is a somewhat arbitrary one. We are confident, however, that principles derived from this more focused treatment of the field of childhood chronic diseases will contribute to the psychological understanding and treatment of other illnesses and chronic conditions as well.

Juvenile Rheumatoid Arthritis

Juvenile rheumatoid arthritis is a connective tissue disease which typically affects body joints with characteristic symptoms of swelling, pain, heat, and redness. Varni and Jay (1984) summarize as follows:

> Juvenile rheumatoid arthritis appears to represent not a single disease, but rather may best be conceptualized as a syndrome of diverse etiologies with three distinct types of disease onset: *systemic onset, polyarticular onset,* and *pauciarticular onset.* Systemic onset occurs in approximately 20% of the patients and is characterized by an abrupt onset in patients who are generally less than 10 years of age, with intermittent fever with or without rheumatoid rash or other organ involvement. . . . Polyarthritis onset occurs in 30% to 40% of all patients and is characterized by arthritis in five or more joints with no evidence of intermittent fever or rash at onset, and typically has an onset in patients older than 10 years of age. Erosive and crippling arthritis is more common in this subtype, with limited systemic involvement of other organs. Upper and lower limb joints are equally affected, including the small joints of the hands and feet, often with symmetrical involvement. Pauciarticular onset, the most frequent onset presentation, occurs in 40 to 50 percent of all patients and is characterized by arthritis in four or fewer joints. Arthritis typically begins insidiously in children under 10 years of age with swelling and stiffness most frequently in the knee. (p. 544)

Estimated point prevalence is 250,000 children in the United States. The annual incidence rate is estimated to be 1.1 cases per 1000 school-age children (National Institute of Arthritis, Metabolism, and Digestive Diseases, 1980). Girls are thought to be affected twice as frequently as boys, and peak onset occurs between the ages of 1 and 3 years and 8 through 12 years (Varni & Jay, 1984).

The etiology for juvenile rheumatoid arthritis is unknown, although genetic predisposition interacting with chronic infection or immunodeficiency disease is highly suspected (Rudolph, 1987). Treatments include pharmacology (aspirin is the preferred drug), physical and occupational therapy, orthopedic surgery, and behavioral/psychosocial services when warranted (Varni & Jay, 1984). Most children (over 70%) are responsive to minimal interventions and can be classified as presenting mild to moderate severity of symptoms. At least 10% to 20% of the children have more severe manifestations, and impairment to functional status is considerable. Physical growth can be affected in those children who do not respond to simpler pharmacological interventions.

Psychological treatments for juvenile rheumatoid arthritis have typically been concerned with patient adherence to treatment regimens, behavioral approaches to relieving recurrent pain, and improving adjustment to functional incapacitation. This disease has received somewhat less attention in the psychosocial literature than other common illness types and, therefore, little is known about disease-specific correlates or outcomes. Much of the psychologically oriented research on this disease has been focused on precipitating factors for juvenile rheumatoid arthritis such as personality characteristics and life event factors. More recently the focus has shifted to the amelioration of chronic pain and improved rehabilitation therapies.

Asthma

Asthma is considered one of the most common chronic diseases in children, based upon prevalence data drawn from multiple sites (Coultas & Samet, 1987). Features of the disease include onset commonly in the second or third year of life with symptoms of dyspnea (difficult breathing), cough, wheezing, and pseudo-pneumonia. The disease can have various presentations for the individual child and there is no typical clinical syndrome. Severity of the disease can change dramatically during childhood with both improvement and deterioration in the clinical presentation common. However, most studies conclude that between

30% and 70% of all asthmatic children improve considerably by adulthood (Perrin & Ireys, 1984).

Much attention had been previously paid to the notion that asthma was essentially psychogenic in origin. This hypothesis has been unpopular in the past 10 years and has been replaced by a model that depicts environmental factors, including allergens and stress, as interacting with a heightened physiologic reactivity in the child. More recently, biochemical imbalances in the autonomic nervous system's control of bronchial constriction has been implicated in the etiology of asthma, although this remains an unproven hypothesis. This hypothesis, however, might help to explain the observed association between life stress and asthmatic episodes in some children.

Treatment modalities have included environmental manipulations such as removal or avoidance of allergenic stimuli, diet changes, pharmacotherapy and immunotherapy. These therapies provide immediate relief of symptoms in most cases but there is no reason to believe they alter the natural course of the disease (Perrin & Ireys, 1984). Risk factors for the disease have included family and genetic variables, maleness, increased *atopy* (systemic reactivity to antigens), respiratory tract infections in early childhood, bronchial hyperreactivity, and the level of exposure to ambient air pollution (Coultas and Samet, 1987).

Cumulative prevalence rates for the full range of asthmatic conditions vary from 8.3% to about 12%, depending upon the specific area of the country. Point prevalence rates have been conservatively estimated to be between 2% and 10% with variation as a function of the age of child, gender, and geographic location. Children over 3 years of age are reported to have significantly higher rates than younger children. Acute-onset asthma attacks are a very common presenting problem in primary care pediatric offices around the country, although the vast majority of these patients are managed adequately without a need for hospitalization. Overall, hospitalization rates for asthma, however, suggest that a dramatic increase in asthma-related admissions for children has been observed during the past 25 years (up to a 300% increase from 1961 to 1981). Coultas and Samet (1987) suggest this could be due to rising incidence rates for the disease, greater severity of the disease overall, or more use of hospitals for asthma evaluation and acute intervention. Some authors argue that limitations in survey and reporting methods have led to serious distortions in the estimated prevalence of childhood asthma in this country and elsewhere (Gergen, Mullally & Evans, 1988).

Mortality rates for asthma in childhood range between 0.1 and 0.7 per 100,000 with higher rates observed in black children as compared with whites. Gergen et al. (1988) argue that mortality rates are increasing due to greater severity of disease than in the past. However, asthmatic children as a group do not have significantly altered life expectancies as a result of their disease except in relatively rare cases. The range of morbidity for asthma is extremely broad with some children requiring very little medical attention or preventive regimen and others requiring frequent attention in both outpatient and inpatient health care settings. With hypothesized increases in the severity of disease in the United States we can assume that overall morbidity will also worsen.

Children with asthma are reported to have an increase in school absences due to their disease and their families show higher divorce rates (Gergen et al., 1988). Impairment of function in an array of areas is possible including restrictions on child and family travel and/or activities, limitation of the child's participation in athletics, and sleep loss that affects diurnal functioning. Also, the medications used for therapy often have associated secondary side effects with mild to moderate behavioral and attentional changes possible. Clinically, such patients can present with panic episodes related to an acutely worsening medical condition and there is some suggestion in the literature that elevated levels of environmental stress can both initiate and prolong this process. Thus, interventions are often aimed at teaching children and parents to make better judgments regarding the severity of asthma symptoms, to teach relaxation and stress reduction strategies, and to achieve more expert implementation of home-based diagnostic and medication protocols. And, as with other chronic diseases, compliance with preventive health care regimens may be low in some patients leading to suboptimal disease control.

Chronic Renal Failure

Irreversibly decreased renal function in children is ominous because most of these patients progress to *chronic renal failure* (CRF) and eventually *end-stage renal disease* (ESRD). Although dialysis and transplantation offer great hope, excellent results are generally obtained only after considerable effort and sacrifice. Even successful transplantation may not correct the effects of CRF, particularly serious deficiencies in growth and psychosocial development. (Rudolph, 1987, p. 1158)

The causes of chronic renal failure include anatomic, immunologic, and miscellaneous factors or conditions which lead to irreversible abnormalities of kidney function. Most children with CRF have obstructive abnormalities of the urinary tract causing hydronephrosis and kidney destruction, though polycystic kidney disease and chronic kidney infections are other causes. The point prevalence of the problem has been estimated at 0.8 cases per 1000 children (Gortmaker & Sappenfield, 1984). The annual incidence of ESRD has been estimated between 1 and 3.5 children per million persons (Korsch & Fine, 1985). Disease onset occurs throughout childhood and into adulthood.

The disease is the result of a consistent and progressive deterioration of kidney function leading to systemic effects on the child and, most notably, problems with excretory functions (Korsch & Fine, 1985). CRF is associated with serious disturbances of bone metabolism and secondary growth retardation. Medical care for the child with CRF can be complicated and involves multiple subspecialties. Often such care produces staggering costs for reimbursement systems and the patients' families. The natural course of CRF is variable depending upon etiology and individual factors including history of interventions and occurrence or progression of secondary problems such as hypertension or infections. Treatments include direct interventions to reverse the deterioration of kidney function or to support the patient during end-stage failure, most notably by dialysis and/or transplantation. Other treatment efforts are directed at associated medical complications during the course of the disease. As with many chronic diseases a multidisciplinary approach across several health settings is required.

> The two most devastating consequences of chronic renal disease in children are the development of bone disease with associated deformities that may prevent adequate ambulation and impaired growth and sexual development with its profound effects on psychosocial adaptation. Assiduous monitoring of various biochemical and radiological parameters of bone disease and prompt therapeutic intervention with vitamin D and calcium supplementation and antacids to control the serum phosphorus level are helpful in preventing and reversing the development of bone disease. This treatment can be administered by a primary physician in consultation with a pediatric nephrologist at a tertiary unit. However, personnel must be available to give adequate psychosocial support in assuring adherence to the therapeutic regimen. (Korsch & Fine, 1985, p. 284-285)

Psychosocial correlates and outcomes of CRF and ESRD include stress associated with the uncertainty of the specific course the disease will take and the often sudden and unpredictable need for intensive and dramatic surgical or mechanical interventions prior to psychological preparation of the patient and family (Korsch & Fine, 1985). The disease can have a direct impact on the child's interaction with family and friends through its effects on urination control and the resulting need for devices to enhance control, and through alteration in normal sexual development and functioning in adolescents and young adults. The effects on physical growth during childhood and adolescence can be painfully apparent and lead to self-perceptual and activity-limiting difficulties.

> The alternation between grotesque swelling, especially around the abdomen and the eyes, and the wasted, puny appearance that results from diuresis undermines children's confidence in themselves as physical persons. In addition, side effects of corticosteroids exaggerate the distorted body image of such patients. (Korsch & Fine, 1985, p 292)

For both CRF and ESRD patients, regular dialysis treatments can be confining and demoralizing, with an array of possible psychological symptoms.

Congenital Heart Disease and Chronic Cardiac Problems

A list of the more common types of congenital heart diseases (CHD) and their estimated diagnostic frequencies is displayed in Table 2.4. The summary prevalence is thought to be between 6 and 8 cases per 1000 births. Disease recognition in approximately 80% to 90% of cases occurs during the first year of life. The etiology of CHD is thought to be through a multifactorial interaction between genetic predisposition and various environmental factors. What is known is that single-mutant genes account for about 3% of CHD, gross chromosomal aberrations account for another 5%, and an additional 3% are known to be due to specific environmental factors such as rubella or fetal alcohol syndrome (Rudolph, 1987). The exact etiology for the remaining cases is unknown, however.

> Congenital means present at birth and for that reason the term congenital heart disease refers to an abnormally formed heart. Any part of the heart may be malformed. Any of the four valves may leak, obstruct, or be entirely absent. The walls between the chambers may be variably incomplete, allowing intermixture of oxygenated and unoxygenated blood in the newborn. (Fyler, 1985, p. 261)

Some cardiac defects are functionally insignificant and those that are life threatening are often surgically reversible, typically during infancy or early childhood. Longevity and quality of life for successfully treated patients with most forms of CHD (but not all) is comparable to that of matched controls in the heterogeneous population. Some sequelae of untreated or unsuccessfully treated CHD include slow or stunted growth (suspected to be associated with the timing of heart surgery), delayed motor development and vascular limitations due to cardiac lesions, and heart rate and rhythm abnormalities (although rare). Neuropsychological sequelae from impaired oxygen flow to the brain prior to surgical intervention (Fyler, 1985) may occur in some types of CHD, though extracardiac problems seem to be more closely associated with psychological and intellectual difficulties than CHD per se.

Management of those children receiving even successful surgical intervention of CHD includes regular and careful monitoring for subsequent problems. This usually involves mildly intrusive procedures and a number of visits to the pediatric cardiologist or primary care pediatrician through the years. It is important to note that CHD and various other cardiac-disease related cases account for about 60% of the patients seen by pediatric cardiologists with the remainder classified as noncardiac disease cases (i.e., psychogenic chest pain, respiratory problems). Some have argued that this latter group actually presents with significantly greater psychological morbidity than more classic CHD patients and, therefore, represents a subgroup which may require greater psychosocial support and expertise.

The initial stress associated with a diagnosis of CHD, and decision making regarding subsequent surgical interventions, constitute two sources of parental psychological upset. However, even after corrective surgery, ongoing subjective distress can be observed in patients, which is understandably related to fears and concerns about the recurrence of heart-related problems, very real postsurgery sequelae, and parent or child perceptions concerning the limitations to normal functioning brought on by chronic or acute cardiac conditions. One important aspect of CHD involves the fact that many parents and children may use the adult model of heart disease as their basis for understanding CHD. Therefore, it is not uncommon to encounter parents who envision their children dying of acute heart failure when this is typically not a realistic expectation. Also, the psychologic effects of a "silent and invisible" defect or disease can be considerable.

Cystic Fibrosis

Cystic fibrosis (CF) appears to be an autosomal recessive genetic disorder typically characterized by pancreatic insufficiency and a chronic progressive pulmonary disease with acute exacerbations. Both these problems result from secretions which have "abnormal phys-iochemical characteristics which tend to precipitate in the duct lumina and obstruct the flow of secretions" (Rudolph, 1987, p. 1420). The disease affects multiple organ systems and can present variably based upon the age of the patient, systems affected, and stage of the disease itself. The point prevalence for the disorder is estimated between .20 and .25 per 1000 persons and the incidence is estimated to be 1 case in about 2000 to 2500 Caucasian births. The prevalence rates are appreciably lower in Black and Asian-American subgroups of the population. Age of diagnosis and clinical onset are variable, although most cases are discovered during the first year of life.

> CF fits into a number of disease categories. It is congenital, it is lethal and like epilepsy, it is largely invisible until late in its course. It can also be extremely variable in presentation and severity, ranging from infants born with intestinal obstruction and respiratory distress to adults who for years have carried erroneous respiratory diagnosis. Most patients survive into their teens or early twenties only to succumb to severe obstructive pulmonary disease. The earlier years are marked with growth failure, respiratory insufficiency, and nagging cough. . . . (Lewiston, 1985, p. 197)

Treatments of CF during the past 35 years have led to dramatic increases in survivability into adolescence and early adulthood. However, survival for those with CF is markedly reduced as compared with the normal population. Over 90% of CF patients are now expected to live past 10 years of age, up to 80% live beyond 20 years, and a small number survive into their 30s or 40s (Rudolph, 1987). Therapies include daily chest physiotherapy to mechanically aid mucus clearance and thereby improve pulmonary function. This is typically achieved through the use of aerosolized bronchodilators and *clap-percussion* techniques (slap on the back). Pancreatic enzyme supplementation and modifications in diet may be required in treating CF patients due to abnormal exocrine pancreatic function leading to problems in digestion necessary for optimal physical growth. Finally, antimicrobials are frequently used to reduce the impact of viral respiratory illnesses that account for most pulmonary setbacks and exacerbations in CF patients.

TABLE 2.4

Incidence* of Congenital Heart Disease

Lesion	Incidence**
Ventricular septal defect	30-50
Patent ductus arteriosus***	10
Atrial septal defect (secundum)	7
Endocardial cushion defects	3
Coarctation of aorta	6
Aortic stenosis	5
Pulmonic stenosis	7
Tetralogy of Fallot	5
Transposition of great arteries	5
Pulmonary atresia	1-2
Tricuspid atresia	1-2
Truncus arteriosus	1
Total anomalous pulmonary venous connection	1
Aortic atresia	1

SOURCE: Rudolph, A. *Pediatrics* (18th Edition). Norwalk, CT, Appleton-Lange, 1987.
NOTE: *Does not include bicuspid aortic valves, which occur in about 2% to 3% of liveborn children.
          **Incidence per 100 children with congenital heart disease.
        ***Excluding preterm infants.

As one might deduce, the progressively deteriorating course of the disease, the routine time and often taxing treatments involved, combined with a decidedly dismal longer-term outlook, make this chronic disease one of the most devastating of childhood. CF care also represents a major cost to insurers and families who must be prepared for many years of repeated treatments, recurrence of acute crises and associated hospitalizations, and high levels of chronic stress associated with the disease and its ancillary effects.

CF also presents the child and family with some unique problems: for example, the special difficulties of the early diagnostic period may continue to haunt families for a long time. Strenuous physical requirements of treatment accentuate normal concerns about autonomy with toddlers. Physical appearance and other symptoms are troubling for the school-aged child. (Matthews & Drotar, 1984, p. 146)

Major psychosocial correlates and possible outcomes of the disease include family dysfunction due to unrelenting stress of the disease and its treatment, problematic self-perceptions of the child as physical alterations accrue and pulmonary insufficiency increases, and the growing dependency of the child on the family and others in the face of normal childhood and adolescent strivings for autonomy and individuation.

Also, there can be striking delays in the child's sexual maturation. Use of psychological denial as a defense or coping style in CF can be quite common.

Diabetes Mellitus

One of the most prevalent of chronic diseases in childhood, insulin-dependent diabetes mellitus (IDDM) has been labeled by some as the *invisible disease* since its manifestations in childhood and adolescence are not overtly visible. The pathogenesis of IDDM is unknown but genetic, immunologic and environmental factors are suspected in its etiology. There is strong evidence to suggest a seasonal variability to disease onset perhaps suggesting a role for viral infections in the etiology of IDDM. It is clear that the destruction of beta cells in the pancreas leads to problems in carbohydrate utilization and insulin production which characterizes IDDM. This condition typically presents clinically with the classic symptoms of *polyuria* (excessive urination), *polydipsia* (excessive thirst) and *polyphagia* (excessive eating). Other possible presenting symptoms indicative of greater metabolic derangement include: fatigue and lethargy, weight loss or failure to gain weight, abdominal pain and vomiting (resulting from *ketosis*, a more serious symptom of prolonged insulin insufficiency), dyspnea, and altered states of consciousness or coma. We make special note of these because initial presentation can range widely from apparently benign symptoms related to increased urination and thirst to diabetic coma and a life-threatening episode. There is some suggestion in the literature on the psychologic adjustment to diabetes that the initial presentation of the disease and immediate health care response can be important determinants of subsequent outcomes and habits in IDDM (Anderson & Auslander, 1980).

Variations across survey methods and samples have rendered a range of prevalence rates between 1.2 to 2.0 per 1000 persons (Drash & Berlin, 1985; Gortmaker & Sappenfield, 1984). Kohrman, Netzloff, and Weil (1987) suggest that up to 1 per 600 to 800 children of school age (kindergarten through 12th grade) are affected by IDDM with a resulting prevalence of 166 per 100,000 children. They also report annual incidence figures of 10,000 new cases diagnosed per year. Diagnosis becomes more common as the child reaches adolescence, with a decrement in incidence after age 12 years. A smaller peak in incidence has been observed around age 5 to 6 years. IDDM apparently affects boys and girls equally but occurs less often in black children as compared with whites. Little evidence exists to support a socioeconomic influence on rates of disorder (Drash & Berlin, 1985).

Reduced life expectancy and the associated physical sequelae of IDDM are not inevitable in most of those who achieve consistently adequate metabolic control through regular monitoring of blood sugar levels and appropriate administration of insulin by injection. The day-to-day care of the child with IDDM requires such blood testing and injections one, two, or more times per day. This regimen must be followed each day, every week, every month, forever. It is a life-long regimen with its foundation established soon after disease onset, typically within the framework and context provided by the initial medical approach, ongoing family processes, the life history of the child and family, and a host of unpredictable events and conditions which can occur after diagnosis. Routine medical follow-up of the child with IDDM should consist of blood monitoring, diet and regimen review, psychosocial support if needed, and ongoing diabetes education tailored to the child and parental capacities.

Known and suspected psychological and familial correlates of IDDM abound since this disease has been one of the most studied in the nursing, psychological, and family therapy literatures (Johnson, 1980, 1988; Delamater, 1985). Broadly-defined family variables include: level of conflict and disorganization, parental psychiatric or psychological problems, marital quality, and others. Delamater (1985) summarizes the research as follows:

> . . . studies of the role of the family in diabetes began with global comparisons of diabetic versus nondiabetic samples, then looked within the diabetic sample using global measures and saw some differences emerge as a function of metabolic control, and finally have recently moved to investigate family interaction patterns specifically related to the disease itself. The results of these studies indicate that diabetes-specific family behaviors are better predictors of regimen adherence than global psychosocial variables, and that conflict, whether picked up by general, global measures or by measures of family behavior related to the regimen, is associated with both poor adherence and poor metabolic control. (p. 349)

Because the psychosocial literature on diabetes mellitus is relatively large and more methodologically sophisticated than other disease categories, we can look to it for guidance concerning the possible connections between disease-specific aspects, family processes, and clinical outcomes in the child.

Variables of interest have included an array of personality character-istics which were at one time hypothesized to predispose the child to, or be produced by, IDDM. Such predispositional characteristics as "depen-dence-independence conflicts, poor sexual adjustment, anxiety, depres-sion, and paranoid suspicion" (Johnson, 1980, p. 97) have been consid-ered. Research has also hypothesized effects on personality characteristics subsequent to diabetes onset which include: depressive tendencies, op-positionality, autonomy and dependency, manipulativeness, and others (Johnson, 1980). More recent studies have examined the impact of diabetes on intellectual capacity and school achievement (Ryan, 1988), behavior problems and psychiatric disorders (Jacobson et al., 1987), self-esteem and perceptions (Jacobson et al., 1987; Johnson, 1988; Delamater, 1985), and the overall capacity to tolerate this form of life stress.

Stress and its role in disease onset has been studied as well with the current view holding that stress may act as a trigger for IDDM, but only through interaction with a genetic component of some type and environ-mental events such as viral infection. Also, there is an emerging litera-ture that suggests that stress impacts adversely on metabolic control in diabetes mellitus.

Hemophilia

The hemophilias are a group of chronic disorders affecting normal blood clotting or coagulation. Hemophilias are hereditary disorders with an incidence of 1 per 10,000 male births and a uniform geographic distribution throughout the United States. Hemophilia, in its severe forms, is usually detected in male infants soon after circumcision when problems with wound healing become apparent, or later in early child-hood when cuts and abrasions do not properly stop bleeding or there is bleeding into a joint or the head. Hemophilia can present in two major forms: *Hemophilia A* (the classic form), and *Hemophilia B* (Rudolph, 1987). The disease was often lethal during childhood prior to the introduction of blood plasma transfusion, but longevity markedly in-creased between 1968, when the median life expectancy for hemophili-acs rose to 19.6 years, and 1974, rising to 30.7 years (Hilgartner, Aledort & Giardina, 1985). More recently, life expectancy for those hemophil-iacs who do not contract secondary infectious diseases has been thought to be essentially normal. Most children are treated with infusions of clotting factor concentrates as bleeding episodes occur, although a small group of children are put on preventive therapies, especially when they have frequent bleeding. The disease is, of course, lifelong and so these treatments continue on a regular basis. Possible medical sequelae of these clotting disorders include bleeding and mild-to-moderate crippling in body joints, increased incidence of liver disease as a result of hepatitis from transfusions, and potential exposure to AIDS through the use of blood product therapies.

Psychosocial correlates and outcomes of the clotting disorders include stress associated with regular treatments and the potential lethality of bleeding episodes, the high financial cost of treatment, and limitations to physical activity for the children themselves. The current rational and intensifying fear of exposure to blood-based infectious diseases such as *hepatitis* and *acquired immunodeficiency syndrome* (AIDS) through repeated blood product therapies has become a major psychological factor in children and families affected by the clotting disorders. Current estimates of those affected suggest that between 70% and 95% of the entire hemophilia subgroup have already been exposed to the *Human Immunodeficiency Virus* (HIV). This exposure may or may not eventually lead to development of the full-blown AIDS syndrome (Andrews et al., 1987), although this development is widely suspected and feared. As of June 1987, 362 hemophiliacs in the United States had been reported to the Centers for Disease Control as having contracted AIDS (Andrews et al., 1987). Eighty-five hemophiliac children (0-13 years) had contracted AIDS as of February 1989 (according to the CDC). At that same time 831 hemophiliacs in the adolescent-through-adult age range had developed AIDS. The percentages and actual cases are based mainly on adults and children who were transfused prior to implementation of more recent safeguards within the national blood banks. It is believed that increased attempts to screen the nation's blood supply has greatly reduced the risk for exposure to the HIV agent (the most current estimate is 1 case per 1,000,000 transfusions), but this continues to be a controversial subject with discussion focusing on the sensitivity of current HIV-related blood screening tests. Some have argued that the rate of HIV exposure is more along the lines of 1 in 40,000 transfusions with an elevated increase in risk for hemophiliacs proportionate to the frequency of infusions they receive (Ward et al., 1988). The risk for contracting viral hepatitis through blood transfusions has been estimated at 10% when using pooled plasma products, and is reduced to about 1% with more careful screening of donors and blood donations and single donor products (Rudolph, 1987). While a more common event, contraction of hepatitis has not brought with it the same psychological impact that the risk of AIDS creates within the current climate of anxiety and panic.

Leukemias and Childhood Cancer

Categories of childhood cancers are displayed in Figure 2.2. All of these have in common the growth of malignant cells in a single or multiple physical sites in the body, leading to destruction of normal cells and associated organs. Combined incidence of all cancers during childhood is estimated at 12.1 per 100,000 white children and 9.3 per 100,000 black children (Pratt, 1985). The leukemias, *acute lymphoblastic leukemia* (ALL; about 80% of all childhood leukemia cases) and *acute nonlymphoblastic leukemia* (ANLL), have an incidence of about 3.03 per 100,000 children under 15 years of age. ALL has a peak incidence between 2 and 4 years of age and there is some suggestion that male children have a 20% to 30% higher incidence as compared with female children (Pendergrass, Chard & Hartmann, 1985). Theories of etiology are many but all involve genetic, environmental, chromosomal and immunologic factors. Viral agents have been implicated in human cancers but evidence clarifying causation versus correlation in humans is lacking.

Until relatively recently the outlook for various pediatric cancers was extremely pessimistic. Improved diagnostic and therapeutic procedures have led to dramatic decreases in mortality rates due to childhood cancers during the past 20 years.

> Whereas the median survival in children with ALL was less than two years in 1967, 60 to 65 percent of children with ALL diagnosed in 1983 will survive for five years and most likely be cured. (Miller & Miller, 1984, p. 119)

More recent estimates would suggest that up to 75% of children with ALL will survive at least five years post diagnosis. The clinical presentation and course of the childhood cancers can vary tremendously. Even in the case of ALL, the most common childhood form, presentation can be variable with some children displaying serious infections and/or hemorrhages, while other children may present with one or more of the following symptoms: "pallor, easy bruisability, lethargy, anorexia, malaise, intermittent fever, bone pain, arthralgia (joint pain), abdominal pain, and bleeding" (Rivera & Pui, 1987, p. 1098). The course of ALL depends primarily on the child's individual response to an array of treatment protocols designed for use with specific types of cancers. In the case of ALL, for example, the primary treatment is *chemotherapy* which involves administration of pharmacologic agents in combination which are known to kill leukemic cells rapidly in the majority of cases. The effectiveness of a maintenance chemotherapy in preventing recurrence of these malignant cells during a 2-to-3 year period subsequent to the initial treatment will determine the survivability of the affected children. Some childhood cancers require radiation and/or surgery on affected organs and tumors produced by *metastasis*, the process of malignant cell spread and invasion.

As one might suspect, the psychological and social correlates of cancer discovery and treatment can be considerable given the life-threatening and often uncertain outlook for many cases, the noxious short- and long-term side effects of chemotherapy and radiation exposure, and the often dramatic impact on the child's health status and day-to-day ability to function. Specific physical impairment, postsurgical sequelae, hair loss and severe nausea associated with chemotherapy and radiation therapy, as well as the effects of frequent hospitalizations, can all combine to create inordinate levels of life stress on affected children and their families. There has been some suggestion that cancers in childhood exert cumulative effects on children and families in direct proportion to the length of illness and incapacitation. Shorter-term psychological responses to the diseases may not appear as dramatic or pronounced as one might presuppose, given the major life upset and anxiety associated with a cancer diagnosis. This finding has derived primarily from emerging follow-up studies of childhood cancer survivors and has added weight to the view that most children and families are extremely resilient in the face of acute disease onset or accidental trauma, and that it is the unrelenting and prolonged process of coping with chronic conditions that largely explains observed psychologic and familial morbidity.

One important clinical point relevant to childhood cancer is that most children affected by cancers are younger in age and, therefore, can present additional problems to the provider of counseling or psychosocial services who seeks to directly assess or treat the child. Because proven methods for communicating with the young child about their disease are few, clinicians and researchers have attempted to apply a myriad of techniques drawn from the child psychotherapy literature and common-sense approaches used in medical settings around the country. As more children have survived cancer we have also seen a concomitant increase in psychological treatment studies and development of measures for younger patients.

Muscular Dystrophy and
Neuromuscular Diseases

Neuromuscular disorders include a rather broad array of diseases classified primarily by site of pathology. Common forms of neuromuscular disease are *anterior horn cell disease* (i.e., infantile spinal muscular atrophy), *acute peripheral motor neuropathy*, *Myasthenia Gravis*, hereditary myopathies such as *Duchenne's muscular dystrophy*, and acquired myopathies. The reader is urged to see Gilgoff and Dietrich (1985) for an excellent review of these disorders. Several features in common across these disorders include muscle weakness and limitation, functional status impairment, reduced quality of life, prolonged medical and therapy costs, and increased psychological risk.

Let us consider *Duchenne's Muscular Dystrophy* (DMD) to illustrate major issues of these disorders. The prevalence of DMD is estimated to range between .03 and .06 per 1000 in children ages birth to 20 years in the United States (Gortmaker & Sappenfield, 1984). The incidence around the world, however, is estimated between 13 and 33 cases per 100,000 live male births (Rudolph, 1987). The disease onset is typically observed after 3 years of age and prior to 4 or 5 years in most children, although many cases can be identified between 5 and 10 years of age.

> Walking is delayed in about half of these patients. When they start walking, they do so clumsily, with frequent falls. Early (muscle) weakness . . .causes the characteristic waddling gait and compensatory lumbar lordosis (arching of the body or back). Toe-walking and peculiar running motions are also noticed early. There is great difficulty in climbing stairs and rising from the prone position. (Rudolph, 1987, p. 1670)

By the age of 12 or 13 years the majority of children affected lose the ability to walk and can only ambulate in wheelchairs. Weakness of the muscles of respiration occurs later in the progression of the disease and most children die around 20 years of age as a result of respiratory failure and infections. Treatments are focused on improving quality of life, since no cure is known (Gilgoff & Dietrich, 1985). These include medical follow-up for neurologic, orthopedic, and pulmonary problems, psychosocial support for child and family, and physical and occupational therapy in the hope of prolonging and promoting functional status.

DMD shares many of the psychosocial correlates and features we have discussed previously. However, psychosocial aspects specific to DMD primarily relate to effects of the unrelenting and gradual deterioration of motor ability combined with reduced pulmonary function. This

% OF TOTAL

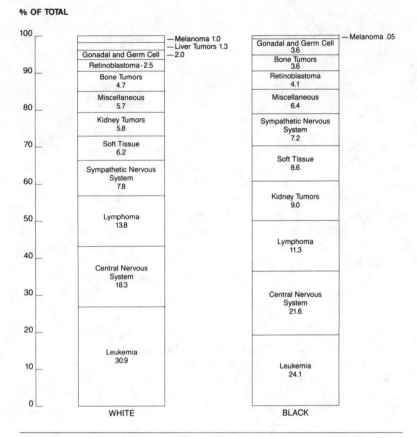

Figure 2.2   Major Cancer Incidence for Children Under 15 Years, by Site, Race, SEER Program 1973-1976.

SOURCE: Pratt, C. B. (1985). Some aspects of childhood cancer epidemiology. *Pediatric Clinics of North America, 32,* 541-556. Used by permission of W. B. Saunders.

disease progression, and a lack of effective medical treatment, has led many physicians familiar with the disease to recognize the potentially great psychological impact of the disease on children and families, perhaps more so than with other chronic diseases during childhood.

Pediatric AIDS

This book would not be timely if we did not include a discussion of the growing problem of pediatric AIDS in the United States and its potential impact on children and adolescents. The current number of documented pediatric cases is just over 1432 children, a number that is based on the Centers for Disease Control records in February of 1989. It is estimated that for every child identified as meeting criteria for AIDS there are between 2 and 10 infected with HIV, the virus that is believed to cause AIDS (*New York Times*, 1988). This number includes children 13 years and younger only; adolescents comprise an additional group at risk for the disease. About half of these children have already died. Recently the federal government estimated that AIDS is the ninth leading cause of death in children 1 to 4 years old and the seventh cause for adolescents and young adults aged 15 to 24 years (*New York Times*, 1988). There is a trend in the emerging epidemiologic literature which indicates that multiple factors are combining to produce a growing number of children with HIV exposure and eventually AIDS. From 1980 through July of 1986 there was a 50 percent increase in the incidence of diagnosed pediatric AIDS in the United States. Children from minority families are more affected (80%) than their Caucasian counterparts (20%) (Ryan, Connor, Minnefor, Desposito, & Oleske, 1987).

> Pediatric cases constitute less than 2% of the total reported AIDS cases in the United States. However, 46% of the known pediatric AIDS cases have been reported within the last 12 months. The National Academy of Sciences (1986) report, *Confronting AIDS*, projected an almost 10-fold increase in the number of pediatric cases from 1986 to 1991, with 3,000 cumulative cases of pediatric AIDS expected by the end of 1991. An estimated 10,000 children will be HIV infected but not diagnosed with AIDS by the end of 1991. (APA Task Force on Pediatric AIDS, 1989, p. 258).

The known modes of transmission for pediatric and adolescent AIDS include prenatal infection from infected mothers, transfusions of blood products, adolescent intravenous drug use, and homosexual or heterosexual activity. It is not known how significantly child sexual abuse will contribute to the incidence of the disease. Currently, the majority of the affected children present clinically prior to age two years since maternal transmission is the primary etiology. Estimates of the number of affected females of child-bearing age indicate that this will continue to be a major problem in the years ahead. The adolescent age group also will probably become a targeted subpopulation for the prevention of AIDS during the coming decades. According to the Centers for Disease Control's AIDS Surveillance Unit, about 350 adolescents (ages 13-19) had contracted the full-blown AIDS syndrome as of February of 1989. Much higher rates of AIDS have been seen in young adult populations (19-26 years), however. This fact, and the suspicion that the time delay between HIV exposure and the manifestation of AIDS can be a matter of years (hypothesized to average between 5 and 8 years for adult patients), combine to suggest that many of the affected cases seen in early adulthood were initially infected during the adolescent period. Thus, adolescent risk-taking and experimentation in drug and sexual areas are likely to be primary foci in AIDS prevention programs.

The HIV infection is a spectrum of diseases since the virus acts to reduce the immunological resistance of the child to a host of common viral and bacterial infections which can result in an array of life threatening medical problems. To date, pediatric AIDS patients have presented with chronic interstitial pneumonitis, progressive neurologic disease, secondary cancers, skin diseases, bacterial sepsis, lymphopenia, and failure to thrive/developmental delay (Ryan et al., 1987). These manifestations of AIDS are secondary to compromised immunologic capabilities, and may cause the eventual death of affected patients. HIV is currently considered a lifelong, chronic infection which can move from an asymptomatic condition to a symptomatic condition at any time. In fact, children appear to have a shorter incubation period for the disease than adults (Ryan et al., 1987). The period prior to death can be particularly tortuous, often involving periods of protracted disability, pain, and dramatic physical and cognitive changes.

As one might deduce, the uncertainty that accompanies a positive HIV screening test, the fears and limitations in daily functioning, and the range of activities which can result are considerable in pediatric AIDS. Also, ostracism and prejudice continue to characterize the predominant societal response to the disease, carrying with them ramifications for the affected child and family. There is little known scientifically about the psychological and familial correlates of pediatric AIDS, but it is clear that, in most cases, preexisting conditions correlated with the infection already place such children at risk (either by sociodemographic, parental, or prior disease/trauma history), and HIV-positive blood testing or AIDS can only serve to make matters worse. It is very likely that we will see increasing numbers of clinical studies of pediatric AIDS patients as the incidence increases and public health policy identifies this group as a top priority in research and clinical service (Olson, Huszti, Mason, & Seibert, 1989). For example, the costs associated with health care services to these children have been estimated to be quite substantial and increased rates of medically unnecessary hospitalizations have been reported. These pragmatic factors, along with the significant threat to children and adults in the U.S., should lead to dramatic public health efforts over the coming decade.

Sickle Cell Disease

This genetic disorder of the red blood cells primarily affects blacks with a point prevalence of .46 per 1000. *Sickle cell anemia*, the most common form of the disease, has an estimated incidence of 1 per 600 live births in the United States. Abnormalities in red blood cell hemoglobin and resulting obstruction to blood flow can produce anemia and structural or functional damage to several body organ systems (Whitten & Nishiura, 1985).

Disease onset is typically identified during the latter part of the first year of life. The clinical presentation is variable with approximately one-third of affected children manifesting severe symptoms of anemia or hemolytic crisis, infections, and/or pain associated with organ impairment. These children require frequent hospitalizations to treat the acute symptoms with analgesics or antibiotics. Typical symptoms include acute and protracted skeletal or body pain, swelling, recurrent infections and fever, and secondary symptoms associated with damage to affected organs. Another third of the children demonstrate a more sporadic and less frequent pattern of symptomatology typically amenable to outpatient management and only occasional hospitalization. The final third presents a rather mild pattern of symptoms requiring much less medical intervention. Yet, these children who vary along the symptomatic continuum can have the identical disease as indicated by laboratory testing (Vichinsky & Lubin, 1987). Bone age and height are often retarded in sickle cell anemia with resultant prepubertal growth retardation and delays in the sexual development of many affected children (Rudolph, 1987). The peak disease mortality occurs during the first 10 years of life (between 7% and 10% of all cases), with life expectancy presumed to be decreased thereafter. Although a median age expectancy has been difficult to document (Whitten & Nishiura, 1985), studies suggest that about 90% of affected children live to age 20 years and beyond.

The psychosocial features of the disease, in addition to many of the more global aspects discussed with other chronic diseases, include the effects of regular or sporadic pain attacks which can dramatically reduce functional status both acutely and chronically. Whitten and Nishiura

(1985) report that their sample of 480 affected children was character-ized by 60% reporting from one to five pain attacks per year and 13% with more than six attacks. Frequency of hospitalization can also be a significant cause of family and child upset since most children (55% in Whitten and Nishiura's sample) are hospitalized from one to five times and about 19% can be hospitalized six times or more yearly.

Seizure Disorders

Epilepsy is not an entity, or even a syndrome, but rather a symptom complex arising from disordered brain function that itself may be second-ary to a variety of pathologic processes. (Rudolph, 1987, p. 1636)

There are several subclassifications for seizure disorders which also vary by the particular course such seizure types show in the individual child. These include *absence*, *generalized*, *tonic-clonic*, *complex-partial*, *atonic*, *akinetic*, and *simple partial* seizures. The occurrence of one seizure in isolation must be distinguished from recurrent seizures over time, which is classified as *epilepsy*. Also, distinctions must be made between *neurogenic* seizures (induced electrophysiologically in the brain) versus what have been called *pseudoseizures*, phenomena which appear similar to neurologic seizures but are actually quite different and thought to be due to psychological or social-situational factors. The diagnosis of seizure type may require the aid of electroencephalographic (EEG) analysis, which may reveal the locus of electrical activity in the brain thought to initiate the manifestations of the seizures.

As the various subtypes might suggest, the overt clinical symptoms for various seizures vary widely, from subtle and barely detectable eye-blinking and staring spells in the child, to total loss of physical control, involuntary movements, verbalizations or utterances. These apparent behavioral manifestations are often accompanied by alterations in cognitive functioning, reponsivity to external stimuli, and changes in perceptual experience. The exact incidence of seizure disorders is not known due to problems in reporting less identifiable forms, but it is estimated to range between 2.6 and 4.6 per 1000 persons (Gortmaker & Sappenfield, 1984). This relatively high figure includes children with only one or two seizure episodes. Some surveys employing more liberal criteria have reported incidence rates of up to 20 per 1000 persons. Age at onset is also highly variable with a peak incidence during the first year of life and additional cases identified at an equivalent rate during the subsequent years of childhood and adolescence. Treatment consists primarily of pharmacologic prophylaxis for one to several years following a seizure event, with ongoing medical follow-up to manage changes in medicine dosage and to address potential behavioral, developmental, and medical correlates or sequelae of seizure episodes and/or the necessary pharmacotherapy.

Seizure disorders merit inclusion in a volume concerned with the psychosocial and developmental aspects of chronic disease primarily because of their relatively common occurrence and the range of psychological and educational correlates and outcomes associated with seizure phenomena. Aside from the obvious psychosocial aspects of any chronic disorder, the neuropsychological, familial, and child self-perceptual sequelae of seizures have been widely recognized in the professional literature, although empirical studies are lacking. Concomitant developmental and social delays have been associated with seizure disorders, as have abnormalities in the development of emotionality and its expression, hyperaggressive and hyperactive behavior patterns, and a higher incidence of learning disorders or educational problems during the school career. These possible difficulties during childhood and adolescence make the seizure disorders a chronic condition category worthy of special mention in a volume highlighting the psychosocial impact of disease.

Spina Bifida and Myelomeningocele

Spina bifida refers to several qualitatively different malformations of the spine, typically identified at birth, which are variably related to more serious neurological, orthopedic, urological, and other problems (Myers, 1984). The incidence is quite high in the United States and Great Britain, occurring in 1 to 2 births in 1000 deliveries. It occurs more commonly in lower socioeconomic subgroups of the population. Survivability estimates have been difficult to make but some reviews suggest that well over 50% of affected children reach the 4 to 8 year age range. Another review reports that up to 50% of children survive to age 20 years (Hobbs et al., 1985), but with increasing physical and mental handicaps as the child ages (Gortmaker, 1985). Treated children clearly survive longer than untreated children and there is much clinical evidence to suggest that regular, multidisciplinary care improves functional status and quality of life for these children (Myers, 1984). An increase in survivability and a growing resistance to passive euthanasia in such cases combine to suggest more affected children will be encountered and cared for in our society in the future (Gortmaker, 1985; Rudolph, 1987).

Myelomeningocele (MMC) is the most commonly recognized form of spina bifida, accounting for over 90% of reported cases. The defect is an opening or protrusion in the area of the spinal column, commonly in the lower vertebrate area, which is typically unprotected by skin thus exposing the infant to increased risk for infection within the central nervous system. Surgical closure of the opening or fragile sac surrounding the spinal opening is performed initially to reduce the likelihood of infection. *Hydroencephalus* (increased fluid-induced pressure on the brain) is also commonly associated with spina bifida. Secondary problems can include curvature of the spine, paralysis, and joint or chest deformities (Myers, 1984; Rudolph, 1987). These deformities, and their concomitant effects on organ systems, can create secondary and serious problems for the child affected by spina bifida, such as impairment in renal and urologic functioning.

Aside from the rather dramatic shock that parents receive soon after their baby's delivery, and the immediacy of major decisions regarding life support and medical interventions, the need for ongoing medical and developmental interventions with such children is an unrelenting source of financial and psychosocial burden to the family. Also, the long-term outlook is not an optimistic one given the modest survival rate and the frequently poor prognosis for functional status. However, it is important to point out that studies of surviving children indicate that intelligence levels during the childhood period are largely in the normal range, but somewhat lower than sibling controls (Myers, 1984). Also, intelligence levels are known to be affected by central nervous system infections, one of the possible sequelae of MMC, so individual history is a factor to be considered.

SUMMARY

Those seeking to understand and/or treat chronically ill children and their families will need to have a basic understanding or knowledge of the features, course, and medical interventions related to each disease type. Disease-specific aspects also help to fill in certain gaps in our attempts to explain the range of responses to chronic illness. For example, specific treatments such as chemotherapy for leukemia or dialysis for renal failure are in themselves additional stressors and experiences which are not shared by children affected by other chronic illnesses. The probabilities for survivability by disease vary, as will the potential psychological effects on the patients and their family members. Compromise of multiple organ systems can accompany certain disease types while others include fewer physical correlates. Also, the known genetic etiologies of various disease types can affect decision making about having more children by the parents of the chronically ill child, as well as the decisions of the child concerning reproduction later in his or her life.

There are somewhat more subtle, but equally powerful, responses specific to disease types. Some diseases are better known in the society-at-large which has led to reduced prejudice and ostracism arising from ignorance. And, several diseases benefit from better organized and publicly supported intervention and reimbursement programs, as compared with equally or more serious illnesses and chronic conditions which receive much less societally-based support and attention. This variability applies to medical care as well where some diseases receive comprehensive, multidisciplinary attention due to a greater awareness of the multiple needs of the chronically ill child, while other diseases receive relatively little attention.

While it is clear that the severity of disease and the resulting effects on functional status and the resources of the family system are essential factors in psychosocial outcomes, they do not fully account for the immense variability in psychological coping that is observed in affected children and families. Even when disease-specific factors are taken into account there remains a sizable amount of variation which can only be explained through characteristics and processes specific to the affected children and families themselves. In the next three chapters we attempt to review and explore these important phenomena, using the theories and methods found in the professional literature on childhood chronic illness as our guide.

3

DEVELOPMENTAL ISSUES

Research investigating the impact of chronic illness on the development of the child and the developmental tasks of childhood has emerged fairly recently within the child health and pediatric psychology literature. With advances in medical care and survivorship has come an increased awareness of the possibly deleterious effects of long-term illness on developmental progress and processes. Alterations in the child's environmental experiences and interactions are an inevitable concomitant of living with a potentially lifelong and life-threatening disease, and these may interrupt or even facilitate normal development in ways which we are only beginning to understand.

A second area of recent research interest has focused on developmental aspects of children's understanding of health-related concepts, their beliefs about the causes of illness, and their sense of control in maintaining health and managing illness. The role that age and, more importantly, cognitive-developmental status play in children's knowledge, attitudes, and behavior related to health and illness has implications for the application of both medical treatments and psychosocial interventions in the care of the chronically ill child. There is growing recognition that educational programs and curricula designed to inform the child about his or her illness, as well as parental and professional expectations regarding the child's compliance with therapeutic regimens, must be guided by an understanding of the individual child's developmental stage and cognitive abilities.

These two broad areas of developmental concern, the impact of chronic illness on the developmental tasks of childhood and adolescence, and the role of cognitive-developmental status on children's health concepts, will be reviewed in this chapter. While this is a relatively new field and there is much need for further research in this area, it will be seen that the existing empirical literature has important implications for both the medical and psychological care of chronically ill children. The effects of chronic illness on the psychosocial functioning of the child and his or her family will be considered in Chapter 4.

CHRONIC ILLNESS AND
THE DEVELOPMENTAL TASKS OF CHILDHOOD

Chronically ill children face the same developmental tasks and challenges as healthy children. However, mastery of these tasks and successful coping with the typical stresses of childhood are made more difficult by the ongoing presence of a disease that can significantly alter the child's physical and mental functioning, as well as his or her interactions with the environment. Physiologic aspects of the disease itself, medications and other forms of treatment, frequent hospitalizations, disruptions in daily life activities, and alterations in family relationships are just some of the factors which may impede normal developmental processes in chronically ill children. An overview of some of the specific developmental issues encountered by children with a chronic illness is presented below.

Infancy and Toddlerhood

The work of Brazelton, Als, and their colleagues has greatly advanced our understanding of the developmental competencies and developmental tasks of young infants (Als, 1982; Brazelton, 1979; Brazelton, Nugent, & Lester, 1987). Als (1982) has offered a theoretical model to describe the developmental agenda of newborns that focuses on the continual interplay between organismic characteristics of the neonate and qualities of the physical and social environment into which he or she is born. She identifies five subsystems of functioning which become increasingly differentiated and integrated as the infant negotiates the transition from intra- to extrauterine life. These systems include the *autonomic* (respiration, thermoregulation, digestion, etc.), *motoric* (posture, tone, movement), *state* (organization and range of states of consciousness from sleep to arousal), *attention-interactional* (ability to attend and respond to environmental stimuli while in the alert state), and *regulatory* (capacity to balance and integrate functioning within the other subsystems). For the healthy full-term newborn, integration and regulation of these systems occur fairly smoothly because the organism is well adapted to the extrauterine environment. The healthy newborn, for example, does not have to expend a great deal of energy or effort to modulate respiratory control and state transitions. For the medically compromised newborn, however, the tasks of maintaining autonomic, motoric, state-organizational, and interactive regulation can become exceedingly difficult and may require extensive and intensive intervention from the environment.

While there are a number of potentially chronic conditions that emerge in the newborn period (e.g., sequelae of severe perinatal asphyxia, neonatal seizures, spina bifida, congenital heart disease), extreme prematurity can serve as a model of how the developmental tasks of infancy are disrupted by a chronic illness. Approximately 1% of U.S. births result in a very premature (less than 32 weeks' gestation) and/or very low birth weight (less than 1,500 grams) infant (Kotelchuck & Wise, 1987). These infants are at risk for a number of complications of prematurity, including respiratory distress syndrome, intracranial hemorrhage, retinopathy, hearing loss, feeding disorders/growth retardation, and developmental disabilities. Approximately 20% of these infants will require prolonged mechanical ventilation and supplemental oxygen and will go on to develop bronchopulmonary dysplasia (BPD), a chronic pulmonary disease (Bancalari & Gerhardt, 1986; Brown, 1987; Nickerson, 1985). Bronchopulmonary dysplasia (BPD) is considered an iatrogenic complication of neonatal medical care, caused in part by oxygen toxicity and high ventilatory pressures, although other factors have been implicated. Infants with BPD may spend several months, and even the better part of the first year of life, in the neonatal intensive care unit (NICU).

At every level the developmental tasks of early infancy, as outlined by Als (1982), are compromised in the infant with chronic lung damage. Autonomic regulation cannot be achieved without the aid of technologically sophisticated medical equipment, including respirators, catheters, feeding tubes, and oxygen monitors. Motoric and state organization are compromised by the infant's physiologic dysfunction and neurologic immaturity, as well as by the highly intrusive and often aversive stimulation imposed by the neonatal intensive care environment (Gottfried et al., 1981; Newman, 1981). Attentional-interactive capacities are limited by physiologic parameters that alter the infant's threshold for sensory stimulation, and by perturbations in the quality of the infant's social-interactive experience. The infant's admission to a neonatal intensive care unit necessarily involves separation from parents, thereby disrupting the family system at a critical point in its development (Barnett, Liederman,

Grobstein, & Klaus, 1970; Caplan, Mason, & Kaplan, 1965; Minde, Marton, Manning, & Hines, 1980; Minde, Whitelaw, Brown, & Fitzhardinge, 1983; Trause & Kramer, 1983). The chronically ill infant's hospital experience is characterized by highly intrusive, often painful, medical procedures, intense and often non-contingent stimulation such as the continuous noise of monitors, ventilators, and staff conversation within the NICU, and repeated changes in caregivers. These events not only interfere with the infant's efforts to master the developmental agenda of biobehavioral organization and regulation as discussed above, but they also disrupt the first critical stage in ego development and psychosocial adaptation as outlined by Erikson (1963), that of basic trust. According to Erikson (1963) basic trust evolves in a world that offers "consistency, continuity, and sameness of experience" (p. 247). These qualities are generally lacking in the experience of the chronically ill infant who requires prolonged and often repeated hospitalization.

Erikson's (1963) conceptualization of the psychosocial tasks of childhood and adolescence has been used by many researchers as a framework for understanding the impact of chronic illness on child development (Cerreto & Travis, 1984; Hymovich, 1974; Lewandowski, 1984; Perrin & Gerrity, 1984; Whitt, 1984; Yoos, 1987). As with the critically ill newborn whose condition becomes chronic, the development of a basic sense of trust among older infants and toddlers is threatened by the experience of painful medical procedures, hospitalization and separation from parents, and the increased parental anxiety and disruptions in family functioning that are brought about by the presence of a serious illness. Lewandowski (1984) suggests that hospitalization is particularly stressful for toddlers between the ages of 1 and 3 years who are negotiating a delicate balance between emerging autonomy and continued dependence on primary caregivers.

Behavioral and temperamental characteristics of toddlers, their wariness of strangers, reliance upon routines and rituals, poor impulse control, and limited ability to verbally communicate thoughts and feelings, together make it particularly difficult for this age group to cope with the stresses of chronic illness. Physical restraint or restriction of movement necessitated by medical procedures, and parental worry and overprotection, frustrate the child's motive to explore and master the environment. At a time when the child has begun to recognize the consistency, predictability, and permanence of people and objects in his or her world, the emergence of an acute crisis, such as the onset of seizures or asthmatic attacks, disrupts the equilibrium of both child and parents. If the illness impairs the child's developmental competencies, resulting in regression or qualitative changes in behavior, the parents must adjust their expectations and alter care-giving patterns. From a transactional viewpoint (Sameroff, 1983), the changed child alters parental attitudes and behaviors which, in turn, affect the child's development and the nature of the parent-child relationship.

Cerreto and Travis (1984) describe the way in which diabetes may disrupt the development of trust and autonomy in this age group. The child's anxiety, brought about by separation from parents, the experience of painful medical procedures, and encounters with strangers who have become substitute caregivers, may compromise the efficacy of therapeutic interventions and the attainment of metabolic control. Sympathy for the child, concern about hypoglycemic reactions or other complications, and even parental guilt may lead the parents to treat the child as "vulnerable," resulting in overindulgence, restriction of activities, and increased dependency on the child's part.

Interventions to normalize and support the development of the chronically ill infant and toddler have been suggested by Cerreto and Travis (1984), Lewandowski (1984), Whitt (1984), and others. These include: 1) minimizing the child's experience of separation by encouraging rooming-in or frequent parental visitation when the child is hospitalized; 2) minimizing the number of medical caregivers in order to increase consistency and continuity of care; 3) providing familiar toys and objects in the hospital and establishing routines with which the child can become familiar; and 4) minimizing restriction of movement, involving the child in normal play activities, and setting appropriate limits.

Early and Middle Childhood

Developmental issues for preschool and school-age children center on the child's increasing autonomy, initiative, and mastery of new skills (Erikson, 1963). During this period there emerges a growing capacity to differentiate self from others and fantasy from reality, and significant advances in conceptual and reasoning abilities occur (Piaget, 1952). The child becomes better able to separate from parents and more involved in peer relationships. For the ill child, particularly the child whose illness imposes limitations on physical activity and social interaction, these tasks may be compromised. As Perrin and Gerrity (1984) point out, the school-age child's widening social network places new demands on his or her capacity to cope with the realities of living with a chronic illness.

Restriction of the child's participation in vigorous play activities, required adherence to special diets, and frequent absences from school due to illness and hospitalization make conformity and acceptance by peers more difficult. Lewandowski (1984) suggests that the school-age child's adaptation to illness is facilitated by: (1) honest explanations matched to the child's cognitive-developmental level; (2) appropriate preparation of the child for medical treatments and hospitalization through the use of educational videotapes, therapeutic play, rehearsal of procedures, and opportunities to handle equipment; and (3) encouraging involvement with school and friends while the child is homebound or hospitalized.

Relationships within the family may also become strained as the child strives for increasing independence from parents while the exigencies of the disease and the necessity to follow strict therapeutic regimens require increased dependence upon caregivers. It is usually during the years of middle childhood that parents begin to turn over to their chronically ill child some responsibility for management of the disease through self-care. Each disease presents its own set of issues in terms of the nature of the treatments required and the level of personal responsibility the child can assume, however there often is an ongoing struggle to encourage compliance and elicit appropriate health behavior while at the same time minimizing the child's sense that the disease rules his or her life. How these issues are negotiated within the family during middle childhood undoubtedly will affect the youngster's psychological adaptation and adherence as he or she enters adolescence.

Adolescence

By far the largest body of research examining the impact of chronic illness on the developmental tasks of childhood has focused on the adolescent period. Psychosocial issues facing the adolescent include adaptation to sudden physical changes and preoccupation with physical appearance, the emergence of sexuality, establishing a sense of personal identity and identification with a peer group, increasing independence and separation from family, developing abstract reasoning skills and formal operational thought, and planning for the future (Blumberg, Lewis, & Susman, 1984; Hamp, 1984; Lewandowski, 1984; McAnarney, 1985; Schowalter, 1977; Siegel, 1987; Yoos, 1987).

Chronic illness may interfere with school attendance, limit the adolescent's level of involvement with peers, and reduce participation in activities such as sports. Delayed physical development or obvious physical disability and disfigurement associated with the illness, or secondary to treatment, make the already self-conscious adolescent even more sensitive to issues of body image and adequacy. The adolescent's need to feel in control both psychologically and physically is threatened continually by the presence of an illness over which he or she often has little control. Challenging adult authority and developing a sense of self often involves teenage experimentation with drugs, alcohol, sexual activity, and other novel experiences, some of which may present a danger to self or others. McAnarney (1985) points out that risk-taking behavior among chronically ill adolescents can be particularly life threatening, such as "forgetting" to take medications or failing to observe dietary restrictions. The transition to formal operational thinking during this period is accompanied by greater attention to issues that are particularly difficult ones for chronically ill adolescents, such as quality of life and the very real possibility of premature death.

The following excerpts from the literature illustrate some of the psychosocial issues that confront adolescents with chronic illness, specifically cystic fibrosis and diabetes:

> At a time when physical growth is rapid, obvious, and expected, the adolescent with CF often faces delays in physical maturation. The effects of pulmonary disease and pancreatic insufficiency result in small stature and lags in development of secondary sexual characteristics. The absence of pubescent changes, coupled with often being the "smallest kid in class" are painful reminders that CF makes one different. Pulmonary complications such as chronic, productive cough, clubbed fingers and toes, barrel chest configuration, and poor exercise tolerance, create obvious physical changes, which draw attention to the adolescent with CF. . . . At a time when healthy adolescents marvel at and become increasingly interested in their body and appearance, the adolescent with CF spends much time and energy attempting to hide the physical stigmata of the disease. Shopping for clothes is painful when one is malnourished and nothing fits; undressing in the locker room with schoolmates is uncomfortably revealing, and developing heterosexual relationships is extremely threatening. (McCracken, 1984, p. 398-9)

> During adolescence, life-altering implications of diabetes become most salient and demanding precisely when the diabetic is least motivated to heed them. . . . Prior to the adolescent years, the parents assumed much of the responsibility for the diabetic health behaviors, and the child's medical education emphasized how "normal" a life-style the child can live with appropriate attention paid to the balance between exercise, diet, and insulin. With adolescence, and the assumption of diabetes self-care, the

teenager is confronted with the reality that there is nothing "normal" about multiple injections daily, constant attention to balanced food and alcohol intake, and monitoring of physical activities. Difference from peers is accentuated. The early adolescent development of an idealized body image is disrupted daily as the teen further mars an imperfect body with needles. . . . The gradual assumption of independence by the adolescent, often turbulent under the best of conditions, is further complicated by even the most well-meaning parental watchfulness, concern, or intrusion into the health care regimen. Experimentation with therapy and rejection of the diet, urine or blood sugar testing, and even insulin, in an effort to control one's own destiny reflects the attitude of experimentation, rebellion, and independence that is a necessary part of adolescent development as they work toward a definition of their own identity. (Cerreto & Travis, 1984, pp. 703-704)

Finally, the issue of adherence to medical regimens becomes a particularly potent one during the adolescent period. Willful noncompliance is recognized as a normal part of healthy teenagers' behavior but becomes highly problematic when it compromises the chronically ill adolescent's health care. Blum (1984) points out that within the medical community adolescents are perceived as chronic noncompliers. Johnson (1984) notes that many of the developmental issues of adolescence, such as peer conformity and the desire for independence, may impinge upon the ill adolescent's health behavior and adherence to treatment. Additionally, in the case of a life-threatening illness, the adolescent may have little hope for the future and therefore little motivation to comply with therapeutic regimens. It is also the case that strict adherence to prescribed treatments does not always make the child or adolescent patient feel better. Maintaining good glycemic control is generally correlated with improved feelings of health in children with diabetes mellitus, therefore it behooves the diabetic youngster to follow a strict regimen of insulin injections, blood glucose monitoring, and proper diet. However, the immediate effects of adherence to many of the cancer treatments, such as radiation therapy, chemotherapy, and surgery, may be increased pain, nausea, and disfigurement, and it is understandable that many children and adolescents would have difficulty seeing beyond these effects to their potential long-term benefits.

Personality factors that may affect patient compliance, such as *self-esteem* (Litt, Cuskey, & Rosenberg, 1982) and *locus of control* (Carraccio, 1987) have been examined within the empirical literature and will be discussed in a later section. Family influences on child functioning will be considered in Chapter 4.

CHILDREN'S CONCEPTS OF HEALTH AND ILLNESS:
A DEVELOPMENTAL VIEW

Piaget's cognitive stage theory has guided much of the empirical work on children's health-related concepts (Bibace & Walsh, 1980; Natapoff, 1982; Perrin & Gerrity, 1981; Perrin & Perrin, 1983; Simeonsson, Buckley, & Monson, 1979; Whitt, Dykstra, & Taylor, 1979; see reviews by Blos, 1978; Burbach & Peterson, 1986; and Gochman, 1985). It has long been recognized that there is a fairly predictable developmental progression in children's understanding of the meaning and causes of disease processes (e.g., Nagy, 1951, 1953; Rashkis, 1965). In recent years researchers have attempted to delineate specific stages of health and illness concepts within a Piagetian framework and to examine the manner in which development in this area is modified by the child's experiences with illness and hospitalization. The following sections, which are again organized by age-related stages, contain a selective review of the theoretical and empirical literature concerning the development of children's concepts of illness.

Infancy and Toddlerhood

Little is known but much has been inferred about the infant's subjective experience of pain and illness. The baby's state of consciousness, which alternates between deep or light sleep, to quiet or active alertness, to crying (Wolff, 1966) is probably the most potent communicator of his or her perceptions of comfort or distress. Variations in infant cry sounds in response to presumably painful stimuli have been demonstrated (Levine & Gordon, 1982; Boukydis, 1985; Wasz-Hockert, Lind, Vuorenkoski, Partanen, & Valanne, 1968; Zeskind, Sale, Maio, Huntington, & Weiseman, 1985), although the degree to which newborns and young infants perceive pain remains a controversial issue (Anand & Hickey, 1987; Lewandowski, 1984). Lewandowski (1984) points out that the neonate exhibits generalized body movement in response to a painful stimulus and it is not until some time between 3 and 10 months of age that pain is localized to a specific part of the body. Memory of painful experiences emerges after 6 months, which corresponds to Piaget's third stage of sensorimotor development, and which is characterized by the emergence of increased differentiation of self from others and the beginnings of intentionality, object permanence, and a recognition of the relations between actions and their effects (Ginsburg & Opper, 1969).

It is the experience of separation from primary caregivers and the restriction of opportunities to explore and master the environment that are the critical features of illness and hospitalization as far as the infant's psychological and emotional well-being are concerned (Perrin & Gerrity, 1984). Blos (1978) states that, "Below the age of 3 years, thinking on issues of causality, especially about one's own pain or vulnerability, is focused on the relationship with the parents. It is the parents' presence or absence that is important" (p. 12). Of course, the infant does not have a concept of illness and does not yet associate physical discomfort, separation, and restriction of movement with being sick. We do not yet know how chronic illness, frequent pain, and prolonged hospitalization, such as that experienced by infants in neonatal intensive care units, impact on the development of the child's health and illness cognitions.

The cognitive development of the toddler is marked by the formation of symbolic functions and mental representations, the understanding of means-ends relationships and, of course, the use of language. It now becomes possible to discuss illness with the child and elicit his or her perceptions of the meaning and experience of pain and sickness. Blos (1978) points out that the child can now understand simple statements about disease condition or treatment (e.g., "This will hurt") but not the reasons underlying these statements. The transductive reasoning of the 2 to 4 year old is such that the child assumes relationships between particular events when no such relationship exists (e.g., "I'm sick because I was bad"). In spite of limitations on the toddler's ability to reason logically about illness concepts, Blos (1978) suggests that simple explanations establish a tone of openness and truthfulness in the adult-child relationship and set the stage for future explanation and elaboration of health constructs as the child matures. Perrin and Gerrity (1984) summarize the toddler's conceptions of illness as follows:

> Toddlers understand illness only as it affects them and interferes with their activities and choices. It is interpreted as something that hurts, something that separates them from the important people in their lives, and something that requires painful and passive medical treatments, frequent visits to doctors, and interferences with play. Because of their magical and egocentric views of causality and their desire to be in control, they interpret illness and hospitalization as events that they somehow caused to happen. (p. 23)

The Preschool Child

The theme of personal blame or responsibility for illness is taken up more forcefully by the preschool child. In an early review, Blos (1978) cited a number of studies reporting that young children perceive illness as the result of, or punishment for, misbehavior. Differences between well and ill children have been found, with the latter demonstrating more self-causality explanations of illness. Again, as Perrin and Gerrity (1984) have noted, the preoperational child's beliefs in self-blame and self-causality in illness may be attributed to the magical and egocentric thinking that is characteristic of children this age.

In one of the few studies that included preschoolers, Bibace and Walsh (1980) examined children's concepts of illness from a Piagetian perspective. Three groups of 24 children each, presumed to represent the three stages in the development of causal reasoning delineated by Piaget, were selected for study. These included healthy 4 year olds, 7 year olds, and 11 year olds, corresponding to the stages of prelogical, concrete logical, and formal logical thinking, respectively. Questions assessing the child's cognitions concerning illness were developed and formed a "Concept of Illness Protocol." Each child's responses were coded according to a category system based on Piagetian cognitive stages. Six types of explanation of illness were identified. Illness concepts among the preoperational 4 year olds fell into the categories of *phenomenism* and *contagion*. From the cognitive-developmental perspective, phenomenistic responses were considered least mature and involved explanations of illness in terms of remote, external, observable events (e.g., "People get colds from the sun"). Contagion, the next level of causation within the prelogical period, is one in which illness is explained in terms of more proximal, but still magical, events (e.g., "People get colds when someone else gets near them"). The preoperational child cannot conceptualize illness in terms of internal, unobservable disease processes and body parts and, as Bibace and Walsh (1980) point out, this has important implications for the way in which health professionals educate and reassure the child about his or her illness. They suggest that it is not until the stage of concrete-logical reasoning that the child begins to recognize a link between external and internal events in the disease process.

In a recent study, Siegal (1988) found that preschool children have a more differentiated understanding of the concept of contagion than Bibace and Walsh's (1980) findings might suggest. Siegal (1988) used a method that involved less direct, prolonged questioning of the child by asking subjects to merely evaluate explanations of the causes of colds, toothaches, and scraped knees as related in a story or by a puppet on videotape. The majority of preschoolers recognized that a cold could be transmitted through proximity to someone with a cold but not by being bad. They were less accurate, however, in their assessment of the role of proximity and immanent justice in causing toothaches. The preschoolers rejected the notion that a scraped knee could be caused by proximity and contagion. The author suggests that the young child's less accurate perceptions regarding toothaches may be related to his or her limited experience with them. The findings indicate that by approximately 5 years of age many children have rejected causal explanations of illness based on immanent justice, at least for illnesses with which they have some familiarity. This does not mean, however, that the preschool child with a newly diagnosed chronic illness, such as asthma or diabetes, would be able to employ the same level of causal reasoning as that applied to commonly occurring illnesses such as colds and scraped knees.

School Age Children

Reasoning about causality in many areas, including health-related concepts, matures considerably during the concrete operational period of development. Blos (1978) suggests that there is a "quantum leap" in children's health knowledge at approximately 8 to 9 years, "a change that reflects the child's improved ability to think in a reality-oriented, causal manner" (p. 15). During this period, the egocentric and magical thinking of the younger child gives way to decentering and the capacity to think about several aspects of a situation simultaneously. In the realm of health concepts, the child begins to understand that disease and illness are active processes that involve some interaction of events occurring inside and outside of the body, although the child's reasoning about these events is still bound very much to concrete, observable phenomena. In the Bibace and Walsh (1980) study two stages in concrete-logical reasoning about illness were identified: *contamination* and *internalization*. Contamination involves explanations that relate some harmful external event with illness in the child through a process of association or contiguity (e.g., "People get colds when they go outside in the winter time without a hat."). Internalization is an illness explanation characterized by the recognition that the illness is localized inside the body, caused by events occurring outside the body, and linked by a process of internalization (e.g., "People get colds by breathing in cold air/bacteria.").

In a study similar to that of Bibace and Walsh (1980), Perrin and Gerrity (1981) examined the relationship between the school-age child's general cognitive development and his or her understanding of illness concepts. As expected, a developmental progression in children's responses to questions about illness, from global explanations, to concrete rules, to abstract, generalizable principles, was observed as the child advanced from kindergarten through eighth grade. The majority of kindergarten children's responses were characterized by magical or circular thinking ("Children get sick by catching a disease") or by stereotyped, often-heard parental injunctions or rules ("By going out without a coat in cold weather"). A beginning understanding, albeit concretistic, of a causal relationship between an external agent (usually "germs") and an internalized disease process emerges between second and sixth grade. However, Perrin and Gerrity (1981) found that there was considerable variability in the quality and cognitive maturity of the child's responses depending upon the nature of the question. For example, children seem to have an understanding of what might necessitate a hospitalization before they understand the causes of illness. Illness prevention was one of the most difficult concepts for children to grasp. In general, the development of illness causality was most highly correlated with concepts of physical causality, although conceptual development in the realm of illness causality lagged behind that of physical causality.

Perrin and Gerrity (1981) suggest that adults' explanations to children about illness tend to exceed the child's level of conceptual understanding. In teaching chronically ill children about their illness it is particularly important to be attentive to the child's cognitive-developmental level and aware of the fact that there is a *decalage* in children's reasoning such that conceptualizations of illness lag behind knowledge and understanding in other areas. The finding that children have particular difficulty understanding concepts related to the prevention of illness has important implications for educating the chronically ill child and improving compliance. This point will be taken up later in the discussion of chronically ill children's health knowledge, health locus of control, and adherence to treatment.

Adolescence

According to Piaget's theory, it is as children enter the period of formal operations, at approximately age 12, that their conceptual understanding becomes more abstract and guided by logical reasoning. The limitations that concrete, perceptually bound thinking imposes on the younger child's understanding of unseen internal disease processes diminish as the adolescent becomes able to reason hypothetically and with greater abstraction (Bibace & Walsh, 1980; Perrin & Gerrity, 1981, 1984; Whitt et al., 1979). Bibace & Walsh (1980) described two categories of response to questions about illness among formal-operational children. *Physiologic* explanations reflect an understanding that the source of the illness lies within the body (e.g., "People get colds when a virus gets into the blood stream"). *Psychophysiologic* explanations are considered the most cognitively mature and reflect an awareness that psychological factors can affect the body's functioning (e.g., "People can get a heart attack from tension and too much worrying"). Although their 11-year-old subjects were assumed to be in the formal-operational stage, less than 50% of these children manifested physiologic or psychophysiologic explanations of health and illness. Indeed, most of the 11 year olds in the Bibace and Walsh (1980) study probably had not yet attained the stage of formal operations. Perrin and Gerrity (1981) found that only one-third of their eighth grade sample demonstrated formal operational thinking which, in the realm of health and illness concepts, was marked by an understanding that "there are many interrelated causes of illness, that the body may respond variably to any or a combination of agents, and that illness may be caused and cured as a result of a complex interaction between host and agent factors" (p. 848). Most of the eighth graders (mean age = 13 years 2 months) in the Perrin and Gerrity (1981) study still retained a very concrete understanding of the concept of illness prevention.

In a study of adolescents ranging in age from 11 to 15 years, Millstein, Adler, and Irwin (1981) found that adolescents most frequently responded to the question, "How do you know when you're sick?" by defining illness in terms of symptoms (e.g., "head throbs," "stomach hurts") although approximately one-third of the sample alluded to psychosocial correlates of illness ("stay home from school," "don't play") which were considered more conceptually sophisticated responses. While adolescents in this study did tend to exhibit more abstract, adult-like definitions of illness as compared with the responses of younger children, adolescents' illness concepts were still predominantly concrete. Contrary to expectation, there was greater conceptual sophistication in the responses of young adolescents (less than 13 years) than in older ones.

In the following sections, the impact of the child's experience with illness and hospitalization on his or her health-related beliefs and knowledge will be explored. Studies examining the interrelations between health locus of control, cognitive-developmental status, and medical compliance will be reviewed.

CONCEPTS OF ILLNESS AMONG CHRONICALLY ILL CHILDREN

It is widely assumed that the chronically ill child's knowledge and understanding of his or her disease will have implications for individual psychological adaptation and compliance with treatment regimens. More specifically, it is often thought that the more information the patient has about the illness and its treatment, the better will be the patient's adjustment and adherence to therapy (Brewster, 1982; Nolan, Desmond, Herlich, & Hardy, 1986). Much of the health care professional's time in treating chronically ill children involves education and counseling about the illness, both in terms of day-to-day management and planning for the future (Desquin, 1986). However, until recently, there were very few studies examining the ill child's specific knowledge about his or her illness, or comparing ill and well children's health concepts. It has been speculated that the experience of living with chronic illness may accelerate the child's cognitive development in the realm of health-related knowledge or, conversely, such an experience may lead to delayed development due to increased psychological stress and the restrictions that prolonged illness imposes on the child's interactions with the environment. As the following review will demonstrate, there has been very little systematic research effort directed toward assessing the relationship between the child's developmental and health status and his or her ability to process and benefit from the provision of health-related information.

Health Knowledge

Brewster (1982) examined chronically ill children's concepts of their illness from a cognitive-developmental perspective. Two aspects of the child's illness conceptualizations were examined: (1) understanding the cause of the disease, and (2) understanding the purpose of specific medical procedures and treatments and the role of medical personnel. Fifty chronically ill children between the ages of 5 and 13 years, representing a wide range of chronic conditions (e.g., juvenile diabetes, asthma, sickle cell anemia, orthopedic conditions, and multiple congenital anomalies), participated in the study. There were between 1 to 5 children within each disease group. The subjects' cognitive level and concepts about the illness were assessed using a variety of tasks based on the work of Piaget, including measures of physical causality, conservation, social role perspective, and specific probes concerning the causes of illness and the role of medical personnel.

As expected, the child's perceptions of illness were positively correlated with cognitive-developmental level. Consistent with the literature on healthy children's illness concepts, there was a predictable, stage-related developmental sequence in chronically ill children's conceptualizations. In the youngest group, children viewed illness as the result of direct human actions, particularly transgressions, and medical procedures were seen as punishments for wrongdoing. At the next level, a physical cause (e.g., germs) rather than personal action was believed to be responsible for illness, and there was an understanding that medical treatments were intended to be curative not punishing. Among the oldest age group, the children began to recognize that there can be multiple causes of illness and that the condition may be the result of an interaction between intrinsic and extrinsic factors. At this stage, the child was better able to infer intention and empathy from health care providers. However, even among the most cognitively sophisticated patients, there was still evidence of the pre-logical attributions of self-blame and egocentric thinking prevalent among younger children, as illustrated by the following remark made by a 12-year-old leukemic patient: "I know that my doctor told me that my illness is caused by too many white cells, but I still wonder if it was caused by something that I did" (Brewster, 1982, p. 361). Brewster (1982) speculates that chronically ill patients may retain magical beliefs in their own responsibility for illness, not out of an inability to think logically, but more out of an attempt to maintain a sense of personal control and as a defense against feelings of helplessness. She concludes by arguing for caution in providing chronically ill children with too much information too soon, thereby possibly dispelling apparently illogical beliefs (e.g, self-blame) which may be serving an important defensive function for the child.

Although children may initially receive the factual information concerning their illness from medical personnel, this information is reinterpreted and reinforced many times by the child's parents. It is important, therefore, to consider not only how the child's understanding of his or her chronic condition develops but also to consider parental knowledge and understanding. While some studies have found a high correlation between mothers' and chronically ill children's diseaserelated knowledge and attitudes, others have failed to find significant relationships within child-parent dyads on these dimensions (Khampalikit, 1983).

Nolan et al. (1986) examined the knowledge of disease etiology and treatment among cystic fibrosis patients and their parents. Cystic fibrosis is a complex disease that presents a wide array of issues related to treatment, prognosis, quality of life, sexuality, and reproduction. Nolan et al. (1986) attempted to determine the extent of patient and parent knowledge in a population of 10 to 21 year olds with CF (mean age = 15.5 years), and to identify specific areas of concern or misinformation. Similarities between patient and parent knowledge were identified and, in general, CF patients and their parents demonstrated better knowledge of disease pathophysiology and treatment than of genetics. Patient performance was predicted by educational level, sex, and parent age, with older (more educated) children, females, and children of older parents exhibiting more knowledge. Significant improvement in test performance occurred over the age of 12 years, corresponding to the approximate onset of the formal operational period. Specific gaps in knowledge, or misconceptions, were identified (e.g., effect of CF on testes and liver, rationale behind vitamin supplementation, health risks of pregnancy among females and sterility among males). Parent knowledge was associated with parent sex, severity of child's illness, and socioeconomic status (SES). The sicker the child and the higher the SES of the family, the more knowledgeable the parent appeared. While mothers performed better than fathers, the number of fathers in this study was very small. Nolan et al.'s (1986) research highlights the fact that CF patients obtain much of their information about their illness from parents and that a high concordance in the area of disease knowledge exists between patient-parent dyads. The authors suggest that it is important to continually monitor the medical knowledge of chronically ill children and their parents. Those families in which there is a significant disparity between parent and child perceptions of illness may be at greatest risk for maladaptation and family dysfunction.

The illness conceptualizations of other family members, particularly siblings, may also impact on the chronically ill child's knowledge, attitudes, and behavior. Concomitantly, the presence of a chronically ill child in the family may alter the well child's perceptions of health and illness. Carandang, Folkins, Hines, and Steward (1979) examined concepts of illness among children with diabetic siblings. Again, using a

Piagetian framework, Carandang et al. (1979) hypothesized that a healthy child's indirect experience with illness, by virtue of having a chronically ill sibling, may create such stress that the child's cognitive-developmental functioning is impaired, particularly in the area of illness causality and treatment. The participants in this study (age range = 6 1/2 to 15 years) were considered to be functioning at the concrete operational, transitional, and formal operational levels of cognitive development based on Piagetian tasks of conservation. Responses to questions concerning the causes and treatment of illness were graded according to the level of cognitive sophistication, specifically the extent to which the child employed concrete, observable explanations versus generalizable, abstract reasoning. Compared to a healthy sibling control group, children with diabetic siblings demonstrated lower levels of understanding concerning illness. Particularly within the oldest group, who had attained the level of formal operations as determined by cognitive pretesting, the children with diabetic siblings expressed less mature concepts of illness causality and treatment.

One might expect that the experience of living with a chronically ill family member would facilitate the child's health-related cognitions, however Carandang et al. (1979) suggest that long-term stress within the family, which is brought about by the presence of a diabetic sibling, has a disorganizing effect on the child's development in the specific area of illness concepts. The mechanisms by which the child's conceptual development is affected by the presence of an ill sibling, particularly among older, formal operational thinkers, are not clear. Carandang et al. (1979) postulate that parental anxiety and the family's focus on specific, concrete tasks associated with the diabetic child's care-giving routine may impede discussions of more abstract aspects of the illness, its causes, consequences, and implications for the future, and this may, in turn, delay the healthy sibling's conceptual development. Adolescents, who are able to engage in more abstract, future-oriented thinking, may be particularly vulnerable to the stresses of chronic illness, whether it resides within themselves or in a sibling.

Jamison, Lewis, and Burish (1986) examined adolescents' perceptions of illness and knowledge of cancer in relation to specific developmental tasks of the adolescent period. Cancer patients between the ages of 12 and 18 years (mean = 15.2 years), most of whom were in remission and without severe physical disability, were compared to healthy adolescents on measures of self-image, health locus of control, and knowledge and attitudes concerning cancer and other chronic illnesses. They

.

found no differences in the self-image of healthy and ill adolescents, which may have been attributable, in part, to the fact that most of the cancer patients were in remission at the time of the study and were not currently coping with the physical symptoms and sequelae of treatment that affect self-image (e.g., hair loss). Cancer patients did express a more external locus of control. Interestingly, there were no differences between ill and healthy adolescents on knowledge of cancer and, in fact, the controls performed somewhat better on this measure. The chronically ill subjects perceived that cancer was less threatening and had a better prognosis than did their healthy counterparts. Intercorrelations among measures indicated that patient knowledge of cancer was significantly related to self-image but not to locus of control. It was hypothesized that the external locus of control orientation found among adolescents with cancer reflected a coping strategy and may have been related to better adjustment. Since chronically ill individuals are forced to rely on outsiders for decisions regarding their health they may deal with feelings of loss of control by assuming an external orientation.

Because of its implications for health behavior and medical compliance, the health locus of control construct has been a focus of attention within the child health psychology literature. The extent to which ill and healthy children differ on this dimension, and its relationship to cognitive level, health behavior (compliance), and psychological adjustment in chronically ill pediatric patients have been debated. Research pertaining to these issues will be reviewed in the next section.

HEALTH LOCUS OF CONTROL AND HEALTH BEHAVIOR

In a study of the psychological effects of illness in adolescence, Kellerman, Zeltzer, Ellenberg, Dash, & Rigler (1980) examined the health locus of control perceptions of healthy adolescents and those with a variety of chronic illnesses, including cancer, cardiac, renal, and rheumatologic diseases, diabetes, and cystic fibrosis. Lower levels of perceived health control were obtained among ill as compared with healthy adolescents, however the findings were disease specific, with greater externality among all of the illness groups except the diabetes and cystic fibrosis patients. External locus of control was, in turn, associated with lowered self-esteem. Kellerman et al. (1980) suggest that the lack of difference between healthy adolescents and patients with diabetes and cystic fibrosis is related to the fact that these patients, in contrast to other chronic illness groups, are able to exert some control

over their illness through specific health behaviors (e.g. dietary management, administration of medications). That is, the authors suggest that
there should be a direct relationship between the level of dependency on
others that the disease imposes on the child and the child's locus of
control perceptions. Kellerman et al. (1980) propose that: "Attitudes of
externality of locus of control, rather than serving as evidence of psychologic deviance, should be regarded as the result of accurate self-perception on the part of these patients. Further work is needed to determine
if treatment approaches that emphasize self-help, such as the use of
self-hypnosis and other autogenic techniques for pain control, have an
effect upon the locus of control dimension" (p. 130).

Developmental changes in children's perceptions of control over their
health, as well as the effects of experience with chronic illness on the
health locus of control beliefs of children and their mothers, were
examined by Perrin and Shapiro (1985). These investigators used the
Children's Health Locus of Control (CHLOC) scale (Parcel & Meyer,
1978) to assess the extent to which healthy children and children with a
chronic illness (asthma, diabetes, orthopedic condition, or seizure disorder) believe in the influence of their own actions, the actions of others,
or chance factors in determining their health. On the CHLOC scale the
child is asked to agree or disagree with statements such as, "I can do
things to keep from getting sick," and "Other people must tell me how
to stay healthy." In general, there was increasing internality in locus of
control with age. Just as children seem to demonstrate a qualitative
change in their health knowledge at the mid-point of the concrete
operational period (approximately 9 to 10 years of age), Perrin and
Shapiro (1985) found that it was around this time that a shift in the child's
locus of control orientation was seen from external to more internal
beliefs. Healthy children (and their mothers) expressed stronger beliefs
in internal control than did subjects in the chronic illness groups. As in
the Kellerman et al. (1980) study, there were some disease specific
findings: diabetic and asthmatic children did not differ from healthy
controls, however children with a seizure disorder or an orthopedic
condition expressed greater externality in health locus of control. In
considering possible differences between asthmatic and diabetic children on the one hand and children with a seizure disorder or orthopedic
problem on the other, the authors suggest that the child's specific
experiences with the illness and the level of reliance upon powerful
others, especially medical professionals, which the illness imposes,
impacts upon the emerging health beliefs of the individual. A seizure

disorder, for example, is characterized by sudden, unpredictable, and involuntary epileptic episodes over which the child has no control and which he or she cannot prevent. The diabetic child, on the other hand, becomes aware fairly early in the course of the disease that there are specific health behaviors he or she can employ to maintain good glycemic control as well as how to intervene when complications arise. Perrin and Shapiro (1985) suggest that the healthcare system itself reinforces external health control beliefs among chronically ill children and their parents through practices that lead to feelings of helplessness and dependency on the part of these families. They propose that:

> Young children should be helped to recognize small ways in which they can take increasing control over their health, but also should be expected to maintain their reliance on significant adults until they are at least 9 or 10 years of age. Children with a chronic physical illness can be expected on the whole to maintain a somewhat fatalistic reliance on chance events affecting their health and a dependency on significant adults, to a later age than do healthy children. As we encourage such children to take increasing charge of monitoring and treating their illness, it would be prudent to help them to develop a better understanding of their own increasing internal control over their health and health behavior. (Perrin & Shapiro, 1985 p. 632)

While it may be assumed that children who express a greater sense of personal control over their health will be more compliant with medical treatments, there has been relatively little research examining this question. Carraccio et al. (1987) failed to find a relationship between health locus of control and patient compliance. A subsample of their chronically ill population, children with spina bifida, were divided into two groups, those judged to be compliant with self-catheterization procedures and those who were not. No differences between these groups on the health locus of control measure were obtained. These findings may be attributable to the small sample size (n=25) or to problems with their measure of compliance (Carraccio et al., 1987).

Moffatt and Pless (1983) examined the relationship between locus of control and several aspects of disease knowledge, self-help skills, adherence, and diabetes control in 156 children attending a camp for juvenile diabetics. A measure of life locus of control (*Nowicki-Strickland Children's Locus of Control Scale*; Nowicki & Strickland, 1973) as well as the health-specific *Children's Health Locus of Control Scale* assessed at the beginning of the camp experience predicted ratings of diabetes control and management skills in the expected direction. In addition, changes toward more internal locus of control beliefs from the beginning to the end of the camp experience were observed among the campers as compared to a noncamper control group, suggesting that this experience enhances the diabetic child's sense of personal control over life events which may, in turn, lead to better coping and adjustment and better disease management.

In an attempt to predict medical compliance among cystic fibrosis adolescents, Czajkowski and Koocher (1986, 1987) developed an incomplete stories task, the content of which focused on medical dilemmas. Responses were coded along the dimensions of compliance/coping, health optimism, and self-efficacy—a measure similar to that of locus of control. Compliance during a routine hospital admission was assessed in terms of participation/cooperation in chest physical therapy and prescribed medical tests, adherence to diet, taking medications, etcetera. Coping behaviors, such as involvement in school/work, openness with peers about the illness, and taking responsibility for medical care at home, were also assessed. Fourteen (35%) of the 40 patients in the study were deemed noncompliant. Coping behaviors, as well as the compliance, health optimism, and self-efficacy scores from the incomplete stories task discriminated compliant from noncompliant patients. The strongest positive correlation was between the self-efficacy measure and compliance, suggesting that patients who believed that their actions could affect outcome were more likely to engage cooperatively in medical care.

Of course with many chronic illnesses perfect adherence to medical regimens is no guarantee of good disease control. For many children, the chronic illness experience involves recurring, often unpredictable acute episodes, complications, and relapses interspersed with periods of relatively good health, control, and stability. There has been very little research examining how specific characteristics of the disease, such as its severity and manageability, affect and are affected by the child's health-related beliefs and behaviors. The complexity of these issues is perhaps captured best by recent studies of children with insulin-dependent diabetes mellitus. In an excellent review, Johnson (1984) discusses the relationships between child/patient and parent knowledge about diabetes, attitudes towards the disease, compliance, and health status. As with other chronic illnesses, children's knowledge of specific aspects of this endocrine disorder advances in age-related stages which affects their readiness to assume self-care. Johnson (1984) reports, for example, that diabetic children are typically ready to inject their own insulin at approximately 9 years of age, but are cognitively not prepared to accurately perform urine testing until the age of 12. She reports that the available evidence concerning the relationship between patient knowledge and diabetic control is inconsistent, as is the relationship between locus of control and metabolic control.

While internality, reflecting the individual's belief that his or her actions will influence life events and outcomes, may lead to greater adherence, Johnson (1984) cites evidence suggesting that this is not always the case among diabetic children. Among so-called "brittle" diabetics, for whom it is very difficult to maintain good metabolic control even with proper medical management, the apparent lack of a contingent relationship between the child's health behaviors and health status may produce so much stress that his or her physical condition worsens, feelings of personal control over health are reduced, and efforts to comply with proper treatment regimens are simply abandoned.

Most often, failure to adhere to treatment is related to lack of knowledge or misunderstanding on the part of the child, rather than willful noncompliance. Johnson (1984) states, for example, that as many as 80% of children may make errors when conducting urine testing. She reports, however, that cognitive-developmental advances leading to increased knowledge and self-care skills are not necessarily accompanied by improvements in compliance, as evidenced by the difficulties encountered by adolescents in adhering to dietary restrictions and other aspects of diabetes management. Further, children who assume the most responsibility for their care may not necessarily be in the best control. Many factors in addition to the child's cognitive-developmental level, such as behavioral and temperamental characteristics of the child, family functioning, and the nature and course of the disease, will influence when and how much responsibility for self-care should be given to the patient so as to optimize health status. Johnson (1984) states that: "Although there is a general tendency to encourage youngsters to manage their diabetes as early as possible so as to enhance feelings of control and mastery, this approach may be in error. Clearly more research is needed to delineate when youngsters should be encouraged to be responsible for which aspects of the diabetes care regimen as well as the importance of parent supervisory behaviors to this process" (p. 516).

SUMMARY

In this chapter the impact of chronic illness on the developmental tasks of childhood, and developmental aspects of health knowledge and behavior among well and chronically ill children were considered. Much of the work in this area has been guided by the developmental theories of Erikson and Piaget. Each stage of development presents specific tasks and challenges, the successful negotiation of which can be interrupted by the presence of a chronic and potentially life-threatening disease. The existing literature relating to the effects of chronic illness on child development is highly theoretical, however, and lacks empirical validation. Further research and, in particular, prospective longitudinal studies are needed to examine how specific aspects of chronic illness, such as age of onset, severity, and type of therapeutic intervention, affect children's passage through the cognitive and psychosocial stages of development that Piaget and Erikson have described.

Developmental aspects of children's understanding of health-related concepts, such as their knowledge of the causes of illness and its prevention, have important implications for professionals working in this field. The extent to which children believe that illness symptomatology is the result of their own actions and their beliefs in personal versus external control of health status and outcome will affect health behaviors which are critical to the care of chronically ill children, such as adherence to therapeutic regimens. Educational programs aimed at increasing preventive and health maintenance behaviors, and strategies used by professionals in communicating with children about their health care, must be guided by a better understanding of children's cognitive-developmental level and, in particular, their health cognitions.

In general, the research that has examined developmental changes in children's illness concepts supports the view that with age come increasing differentiation and internalization of the child's understanding of illness and an increased sense of personal control over health. Attempts to link specific developmental changes in health-related knowledge to changes in the structure of intelligence, as described by Piaget, have been fairly successful, although reasoning in the domain of health and illness tends to be less advanced than in other areas (e.g., physical causality). Piaget used the term decalage to describe such variations in children's applications of certain cognitive schemes to specific content areas. The available data suggest that many adolescents still hold very concrete views concerning the nature and causes of illness, and children in general have difficulty grasping concepts related to health prevention. Health locus of control and preventive health behavior become particularly important issues for chronically ill children who are expected to assume more and more responsibility for their health care with increasing age.

Chronically ill children and their siblings, simply by virtue of their increased experience with illness and medicine, do not appear to have advanced understanding of illness concepts. Further, level of knowledge about health and illness is not directly linked to either compliance or disease control. There is still much to be learned about the interrelations between child, family, and environmental factors on the one hand, and disease-specific treatment task demands on the other, in affecting children's health behavior and adherence to treatment.

Not surprisingly, within many chronic illness groups children express an external health locus of control orientation. This may vary, however, as a function of the particular chronic condition and the extent to which the child/patient is able to manage the course of the disease by engaging in specific health behaviors. Just as the level of health knowledge does not always relate to health behavior among chronically ill children, health locus of control has not been found to be consistently related to medical compliance. Findings vary, again, depending upon the particular disease group studied.

Much of the literature in this area is limited by the correlational nature of the research designs that have been employed. It is not clear whether an external locus of control orientation leads to decreased compliance and consequently more medical complications, or whether a difficult to manage disease, even with good adherence to therapy, reduces feelings of personal control over health, thereby compromising efforts to elicit patient compliance. Further research is needed to examine what aspects of the disease itself, disease-specific caregiving task demands, and developmental and personality characteristics of the child affect chronically ill children's health behavior and readiness for self-care.

4

PSYCHOSOCIAL
FUNCTIONING

OVERVIEW

As noted earlier in this book, there is increasing evidence that, contrary to reports of 10 or 20 years ago, most children with chronic illness do not manifest psychological disturbance or maladjustment (Blumberg et al., 1984; Creer, 1987; Drotar et al., 1981; Kellerman et al, 1980; Koocher & O'Malley, 1981; McCracken, 1984; Offer, Ostrov, & Howard, 1984; Orr, Weller, Satterwhite, & Pless, 1984; Stabler, 1988; Zeltzer, Kellerman, Ellenberg, Dash, & Rigler, 1980, Zeltzer, LeBaron, & Zelter, 1984). In addition, efforts to identify distinctive behavioral features or personality characteristics within specific chronic illness groups, akin to the Type A behavior pattern associated with coronary heart disease, have not met with success. For example, the corpus of data fail to support the view that there is a characteristic "diabetic personality" (Cerreto & Travis, 1984; Johnson, 1984; Rodin, 1983), "juvenile arthritis personality" (Varni & Jay, 1984), or "asthmatic personality" (Creer, 1987). Similarly, while earlier work, often based on retrospective data, focused on presumed psychopathology within families of chronically ill children, conceptual and methodological advances in research design, such as use of direct observation and appropriate control groups, have led to a recognition of the remarkable resiliency and coping capacities of these families (Hobbs et al., 1985; Stabler, 1988).

Although major psychiatric disturbance is not common among children with chronic illness, as noted in Chapter 2, this population is at increased risk for mental health and adjustment problems (Armstrong, Wirt, Nesbit, & Martinson, 1982; Cadman et al., 1987; Daniels et al.,

1987; Drotar & Bush, 1985; Pless & Roghmann, 1971; Wallander, Varni, Babani, Banis, & Wilcox, 1988). The magnitude of this risk varies from study to study, reflecting definitional and methodological inconsistencies. Findings from the Ontario Child Health Study (Cadman et al., 1987) indicated that psychosocial adaptation was significantly affected by the level of functional disability imposed by the illness. In that study, *social isolation* and *school adjustment problems* were more prevalent among children with both chronic illness and functional limitations than either a chronic illness only or healthy control group.

Breslau (1985) confirmed earlier findings that psychiatric risk associated with physical disability increases when there is brain involvement. She examined children with cystic fibrosis, cerebral palsy, myelodysplasia, multiple physical handicaps, and a healthy comparison group. On the *Psychiatric Screening Inventory*, a maternal report questionnaire consisting of 35 items comprising 7 subscales (Self-Destructive Tendencies, Mentation Problems, Conflict with Parents, Regressive-Anxiety, Fighting, Delinquency, and Isolation), disabled children scored significantly higher than controls in the areas of Mentation Problems, Conflict with Parents, Regressive-Anxiety, and Isolation. Cystic fibrosis patients demonstrated significantly less psychopathology than children in the other diagnostic groups who had brain involvement, and they did not differ from controls on the Mentation Problems and Isolation subscales. Children with brain involvement demonstrated particularly marked disturbance in these two domains. Risk of psychiatric impairment was directly related to level of mental retardation. Breslau (1985) suggests that increased problems in the areas of Conflict with Parents and Regressive-Anxiety, found within all diagnostic groups, reflect a common response to chronic physical illness irrespective of the specific type of disorder. As in the Ontario Child Health Study (Cadman et al., 1987) these findings highlight the association between social isolation, chronic disability, and increased psychiatric risk. However, contrary to Cadman et al. (1987), Breslau (1985) did not find that severity of disability, assessed in terms of activities of daily living, was related to risk of psychopathology when type of condition and mental retardation were controlled.

Level of impairment in daily living and persistence of chronic disease were related to risk of psychosocial maladjustment in a longitudinal study of chronically ill children followed into adolescence (Orr et al., 1984). Interestingly, there was no relationship between early health status and later psychosocial functioning, leading the authors to conclude that, "The simple presence of a chronic medical problem 8 years earlier did not seem to place the child at increased risk for subsequent psychosocial problems" (Orr et al., 1984, p. 155). At follow-up, psychosocial maladaptation appeared in those individuals who had moderate or severe disability that had persisted into adolescence and young adulthood, manifested by disturbed social relations, underachievement, poor home life, and lack of future planning. Pless and Roghmann (1971) also found that the risk of psychosocial and behavioral pathology in chronically ill children was related to the duration of the disorder and, to a lesser extent, its severity as measured by interference with activities of daily living.

There is some disagreement within the chronic illness literature concerning the role of severity of disease in affecting psychosocial adjustment. Drotar and Bush (1985), in an extensive review, note that "disease severity based on objective physical criteria may not be as important as personal perceptions of illness in mediating adjustment" (p. 518). Drotar et al. (1981) studied cystic fibrosis patients, their healthy siblings, children with other chronic illnesses such as asthma and pulmonary disease, and healthy controls. Adjustment scores based on behavioral checklists completed by parents and teachers did not correlate with measures of physical status, with the exception that greater physical impairment was associated with parental ratings of social withdrawal. Drotar et al. (1981) do note that the CF children in their study were sufficiently healthy to attend school regularly and engage in adequate levels of activity at home. These results do not, therefore, dispute findings reported earlier that when physical impairment is so severe that it limits activities of daily life, social withdrawal, isolation and psychosocial problems arise.

Assessing psychopathology in chronically ill patients presents a number of problems of definition and classification. Several investigators in this field (e.g., Drotar & Bush, 1985; Orr et al., 1984; Van Dongen-Melman & Sanders-Woudstra, 1986) have pointed to the limitations of applying psychiatric diagnoses to chronically ill children whose behavioral symptomatology, while perhaps pathological in a healthy population, is adaptive or at least appropriate given the circumstances of their illness and life experience. A child who is suffering the ravages of severe cystic fibrosis or the ordeal of cancer and its potentially debilitating and painful treatments, the brittle diabetic who, even in spite of good medical care, often does not feel well because blood glucose levels are too high or too low, the child with juvenile rheumatoid arthritis or sickle cell disease who often experiences physical pain, the hemophiliac who cannot participate in normal play activities or sports for fear of injury, all have good reason to feel dysphoric. Similarly, social withdrawal, and particularly avoidance of peers, can be viewed as a normal response to the presence of disfigurement and physical discomfort resulting from chronic illness.

The use of psychological *denial* by chronically ill children and their families is a good example of an adaptive coping strategy that in healthy populations is generally perceived to be inappropriate or maladaptive. Adaptive denial involves maintaining a positive future outlook, focusing on the concrete tasks of daily life, avoiding thoughts of illness, and believing in one's own survivability even in the face of a severe and life-threatening disease (Blumberg et al., 1984; Van Dongen-Melman & Sanders-Woudstra, 1986; Zeltzer et al., 1980, 1984). Zeltzer et al. (1980, 1984) reported that more than 95% of adolescents with cancer felt that things would get better even though approximately one-third of this group had relapsed at the time of study, and many of those died within 2 weeks to 6 months later. Researchers working in the field of childhood chronic illness must come to terms with the fact that in assessing psychiatric function and dysfunction it may be inappropriate to hold these children to the same clinical standards that are applied to their healthy counterparts.

The vast inconsistencies and confusion in the literature pertaining to the rate of psychiatric or behavioral symptomatology among chronically ill children are easily explained by sampling differences and variability in methods and instruments used to assess psychopathology or psychosocial maladjustment. In addition, medical advances, which in the case of some diseases such as cancer are occurring at a rapid rate, are changing the course, treatment, and outcome for afflicted children. This, in turn, will impact on psychosocial functioning thereby making earlier findings obsolete. Because of ongoing developments in medical care, Hobbs et al. (1985) have stated that researchers studying the psychological consequences of childhood chronic illness are facing a "moving target."

As a general statement, it can be said that there is wide variability in the level of psychosocial functioning attained by children with chronic physical illness. Some children with mild disease will encounter severe problems of adjustment while others, with more serious, life-threatening disease, will cope extraordinarily well (Drotar & Bush, 1985). To move beyond global comparisons of chronically ill and healthy children, which have demonstrated some measure of increased mental health risk in the former, there is much need for further research to identify specific subpopulations of chronically ill children who are at risk, to identify specific child and family variables that place some children at increased risk, to delineate more explicitly the nature of the problems encountered, and to uncover correlates of effective adaptation and coping.

Before proceeding to a review of the literature pertaining to specific aspects of psychological functioning among chronically ill children, adolescents, and their families, mention should be made of two approaches to the study of psychosocial adaptation in the chronically ill. Drawing from the work of Pless and Pinkerton (1975), Stein and Jessop (1982, 1984a, 1984b; Jessop & Stein, 1985) have proposed a noncategorical approach to chronic childhood illness. They suggest that health issues pertaining to chronically ill children and their families cross specific diagnostic boundaries; that is, there are many common features of both adjustment and reaction to illness among differing chronic disease groups. These investigators feel that a broader conceptual framework, which is not disease specific, will enhance professionals' understanding of the impact of chronic illness on the "total life experience" of chronically ill children and their families and will improve quality of care. They advocate use of noncategorical measures, such as *functional status* of the child, based on normal social role performance, and *index of burden* on the family, which assesses generic features of illness irrespective of disease category (e.g., care-giving task demands, illness-imposed disruption in family routine, and level of child dependency due to inability to perform age-appropriate activities of daily living). Using this model, Stein and Jessop (1984; Jessop & Stein, 1985) have demonstrated that the functional status of children from diverse chronic illness categories is related to their psychological adjustment, psychiatric symptoms in mother, and impact of illness on the family.

In support of the individual-specific as opposed to disease-specific approach, Stein and Jessop (1982) state that:

> One result of defining chronic illness noncategorically is that physical differences between people are seen in a less stigmatizing way. One can begin to look at minor and major differences in health status as points along a continuum from the completely healthy to the severely ill. It is an attempt to break out of gross categorizations of people (for example, "asthmatic," "diabetic," "cystic"), which are labels intended to designate discrete groups. In terms of life chances, psychological, social, and

medical variables, more variability seems to occur within each of these groups than between them. (p. 361)

In general, researchers who do not find differences on psychological variables between chronic illness groups (e.g., Cassileth et al., 1984; Wallander et al., 1988) tend to support the noncategorical view, while those who do find differences (e.g., Cadman et al., 1987; Steinhausen et al., 1983) recommend the use of models that are both disease specific and differentiated with respect to psychiatric diagnosis. An advantage of the noncategorical view is that it focuses on universal features of psychosocial adaptation among children and families and avoids some of the pitfalls mentioned earlier in using traditional psychiatric nosologies derived from physically healthy populations. There are, however, unique features of each chronic illness, such as the type of therapeutic regimen required, whether the disease imposes sensory limitations, is associated with chronic pain and/or disfigurement, involves repeated hospitalizations, affects central nervous system functioning, is associated with early or late onset, and so on (Rae-Grant, 1985), which undoubtedly interact with personality characteristics of the individual in affecting psychological and behavioral adaptation. The following review of specific aspects of psychosocial functioning in chronically ill children and their families, which is by necessity highly selective and focused on the most recent reviews of literature and empirical studies, will demonstrate the need for, and use of, both disease-specific and noncategorical approaches in this area of research.

COGNITIVE FUNCTIONING AND ACADEMIC PERFORMANCE

There are many paths through which chronic illness may affect a child's intellectual and academic functioning. For example, disease-related insults to the central nervous system resulting in cognitive delays or deficits are associated with a number of chronic conditions, such as seizure disorder, spina bifida, neurofibromatosis and, of most recent concern, pediatric acquired immunodeficiency syndrome (AIDS). Cognitive deficits secondary to medications and other therapeutic interventions may occur with diseases such as asthma and cancer. Chronic pain or physical fatigue, often experienced by patients with sickle cell anemia, leukemia, arthritis, cystic fibrosis, and congenital heart disease, may limit the child's ability to concentrate and process information in school. In addition, the psychological stress of living with a chronic condition, frequent school absences due to illness and hospitalization, and disease-related restrictions on the child's experiences and interactions with the environment may interfere with the normal course of cognitive and academic development. It should be noted that the majority of children with chronic illness do not have intellectual impairments (Hobbs et al., 1985), and if there are disease-related effects on cognitive-intellectual functioning these may not always be negative. Mearig (1985), for example, cites evidence that chronic illness may sometimes produce cognitive benefits, perhaps secondary to the child's increased interactions with and attention from adults.

To illustrate some of the mechanisms by which childhood illness may impact directly or indirectly on intellectual functioning, recent research concerning the neuropsychological concomitants of several diseases will be discussed below. These diseases are chosen simply to highlight issues in the study of chronic illness effects on cognitive functioning. The discussion is deliberately selective rather than exhaustive and the reader is referred elsewhere for a more comprehensive review (e.g., Mearig, 1985).

Cognitive Deficits Associated with Disease-Specific Brain Dysfunction

Recent evidence suggests that in certain chronic illnesses that are not commonly considered to be brain related, such as diabetes and sickle cell anemia, the pathophysiology of the disease may produce subtle neuropsychological deficits in children. For example, early onset (less than 5 years of age) as opposed to late onset diabetes mellitus has been found to be associated with lower scores on general tests of neurobehavioral functioning (Ryan, 1988) and, in particular, visuospatial abilities (Rovet, Ehrlich, & Hoppe, 1988). Rovet et al. (1988) also found that school difficulties and special educational placement were more common in early onset diabetic children. These results do not appear to be attributable to the duration of disease or to recent metabolic control. Rather, it has been hypothesized that the greater incidence of hypoglycemic seizures or coma in younger diabetic children, and the hypersensitivity of the immature brain to physiological disturbances, may produce such cognitive impairments. Ryan (1988) cautions, however, that findings to date are highly tentative and further research is needed to explore the interrelations of biomedical, psychosocial, and organismic factors that may affect the neurobehavioral functioning of the diabetic child.

Other evidence of subtle neuropsychological deficits in a condition which is not typically associated with brain involvement comes from recent work on childhood sickle cell anemia. Fowler et al. (1988) found that although school age children with SCA did not differ from healthy, matched controls on measures of cognitive-intellectual ability, they did demonstrate deficits in visual-motor integration skills, attentional abilities, and academic achievement. These investigators suggest that subclinical vascular or metabolic CNS insults associated with sickle cell disease may contribute to learning problems in some children. Again, the results are based on a small number of subjects and further research and replication are needed.

More direct evidence of brain injury potentially leading to neuropsychologic dysfunction is found, of course, among victims of childhood brain tumors. Mulhern, Crisco, and Kun (1983) have reviewed this literature and report that children with both supratentorial and infratentorial tumors, and children treated with cranial irradiation, are at increased risk of cognitive impairment, although there is great variability across studies in the incidence and severity of such deficits. Mulhern et al. (1983) cite the paucity of data and methodological flaws in explaining the lack of conclusive evidence concerning the relationships between age at diagnosis, treatment modality and dosage, and tumor location in predicting neuropsychologic sequelae.

Finally, mention should be made of a newly emerging and rapidly growing population of children with chronic illness affecting neurodevelopmental functioning: pediatric AIDS patients. In the majority of cases, the AIDS virus has been transmitted to the fetus in utero by an infected mother who presents with adult risk factors of IV drug abuse and/or prostitution or promiscuity. Clinical manifestation of the disease generally occurs by 2 years of age (Barbour, 1987). Several studies have now documented both static and progressive neurodevelopmental dysfunction in children with AIDS, including secondary microcephaly, cognitive deficits, disorders of tone and movement, and loss of acquired sensorimotor and language milestones. These are most likely the result of CNS infections and cerebral atrophy (Belman, Diamond et al., 1988; Belman, Ultmann et al., 1985; Epstein et al., 1985; Ultmann et al., 1985). As Ultmann et al. (1985) point out, there are many factors in addition to direct CNS involvement, such as prenatal exposure to drugs, perinatal complications secondary to poor prenatal care, chronic illness and failure to thrive, and psychosocial disturbances in the environments into which these children are born, that may predispose them to neurodevelopmental abnormalities. As we noted in Chapter 2, the numbers of children admitted to pediatric units for treatment of AIDS will increase dramatically over the next several years, and the multiplicity of medical, developmental, and psychosocial problems confronting this new population of chronically ill children will present a great challenge to professionals working in the fields of medicine, nursing, pediatric psychology, and social services.

Treatment-Related Cognitive Deficits

Neuropsychological sequelae of therapeutic medications and other medical interventions have been associated with some chronic illnesses, most notably asthma and cancer. In a discussion of the psychological aspects of childhood asthma, Creer (1987) reviews a number of studies which report neuropsychological impairment in asthmatic children as compared to matched controls. Specific deficits have been found in the areas of visual-spatial abilities and memory. There is some controversy in the literature concerning the extent to which these problems are attributable to hypoxic episodes resulting from severe asthmatic attacks or whether such findings reflect the deleterious effects of the medicines, particularly *corticosteroids* and *theophylline*, which are prescribed for many of these patients. This has stimulated research on the neurobehavioral effects of asthma medications. Theophylline administration has been associated with decreased performance on memory tests and parental report of increased irritability, restlessness, sleep problems, and depression in asthmatic children (Creer, 1987).

Interest in the short- and long-term effects of medical treatments applied to pediatric cancer patients has increased with the relatively recent and quite dramatic improvements in survival within this population. Children with leukemia often receive prophylactic CNS therapy as well as systemic chemotherapy. The effects of these interventions on neuropsychological and academic functioning have been examined in a number of recent reports (Copeland et al., 1988; Heukrodt et al., 1988; Trautman et al., 1988).

In a study of 28 long-term survivors of acute lymphoblastic leukemia (ALL), all of whom were at least 4 years post-diagnosis and currently in remission, Heukrodt et al. (1988) found that 50% of these patients had learning disabilities based on performance on the *Wide Range Achievement Test*. In addition, 5 of 14 patients (36%) who had been treated for solid tumors outside the CNS were considered learning disabled. Both the ALL and solid tumor groups showed electrophysiological evidence of slowed cognitive processing time, although these groups had been treated with differing combinations of systemic and intrathecal chemotherapy and cranial and non-CNS radiation. These investigators conclude that both radiation and chemotherapy have potentially neurotoxic effects, even if treatment has not been applied directly to the CNS.

There are as yet many unanswered questions concerning the effects of different modalities and combinations of treatment, age at diagnosis, and duration of therapy on the neuropsychological functioning of children with cancer. Within this literature sample sizes are usually small and often there are no measures of premorbid and pre-treatment functioning. Findings to date must, therefore, be considered tentative. There does appear to be accumulating evidence, however, that cancer treatments produce at least subtle neuropsychological deficits that may impact on the academic achievement of these children.

SOCIAL-EMOTIONAL FUNCTIONING

Self-Esteem and Social Adjustment

As noted in Chapter 3, the presence of a chronic illness threatens the child's successful negotiation of normal developmental tasks, disrupts activities of day-to-day life, and may even affect physical appearance. Concern regarding the impact of such disruptions on the child's emerging self-concept has led some researchers to examine self-perceptions and social adjustment in this population. Most of these studies have focused on chronically ill adolescents.

The research mentioned earlier by Kellerman et al. (1980) was one of the first large-scale studies of psychological functioning in chronically ill adolescents. Physically healthy junior high and high school students (N=349) were compared to chronically ill adolescents (N=168) on a number of measures including trait anxiety, self-esteem and, as reported previously, health locus of control. Statistically significant differences between the healthy and ill adolescents on the anxiety and self-esteem measures did not obtain, nor were there differences between the various illness groups.

Zeltzer et al. (1980) examined these data further using an illness-impact questionnaire that focused on issues of family relations, school and peer activities, independence, effects of treatment, and social and sexual functioning. They found that the major disruptions brought about by illness, as these adolescents perceived them, involved restrictions of freedom and disruptions in peer and family relations. Some interesting disease-specific findings emerged, with more disruptions of body image secondary to disease and treatment reported by the rheumatology and cancer patients. Treatment-related problems were most pronounced within the cancer groups, many of whom felt that the treatment was worse than the disease. Diabetic adolescents received the lowest total impact of illness scores and they reported less illness-related peer disruptions than did their healthy counterparts. The impact of illness on physical appearance was greater in females than males. Adolescents' perceptions of the degree of impact of illness on their lives was inversely related to self-esteem.

Perhaps the most interesting finding to emerge from the Zeltzer et al. (1980) study was the lack of difference between healthy and chronically ill adolescents on the total impact of illness measure. That is, the healthy teen-agers, 30% of whom reported current illnesses such as allergies, colds, headaches, sinus problems, and so on, felt that their illnesses were as disruptive as those occurring in the chronic illness group. The authors hypothesize that for youngsters who are usually well minor illness can be perceived as a major disruption, while chronically ill individuals may deemphasize and even deny the significance of illness except in the most severe circumstances. The experience of chronic illness and the need for ongoing medical treatment may actually strengthen, up to a point, the child's ability to deal with the disruptions in every day life which the illness imposes.

Subsequent studies (e.g., Offer et al., 1984; Simmons et al., 1985) have confirmed the earlier findings of Kellerman and Zelter concerning self-esteem in chronically ill youngsters, although the Offer et al. (1984) study did find lowered self-image among cystic fibrosis adolescents. In a review of the literature, McAnarney (1985) concludes that, overall, controlled studies of large cohorts of adolescents have failed to demonstrate that chronically ill teenagers have lower self-esteem; however, findings vary as a function of population characteristics and the specific nature of the disease. In terms of social maturation, she reports that chronically ill adolescents tend to be more dependent on family and less advanced in the development of sexuality than their healthy counterparts.

Although severe social and behavioral maladaptation in chronically ill children is the exception rather than the rule, there is a continuing need for researchers in this field to identify organismic and environmental parameters that place some of these children at increased risk for problems of adjustment. The work of Koocher and O'Malley (1981) with cancer patients is instructive in this regard. They looked at the psychosocial adjustment of 117 individuals who had survived childhood cancer. The patients all had been diagnosed and treated for childhood malignancy at least 5 years earlier and were disease-free at the time of the study. Fifty-three percent of the childhood cancer survivors showed no evidence of maladjustment. When compared with a small group (n=22) of people who had been successfully treated earlier for other childhood chronic illness, in which there was little likelihood of disease recurrence, the former cancer patients showed more maladjustment and reported lower levels of satisfaction. Factors that distinguished adjusted from maladjusted groups included family income, having a form of cancer which required a short treatment course and in which there were few permanent side effects, being relapse or recurrence-free, and having disease onset during infancy or early childhood.

Depression

The study by Koocher and O'Malley (1981) reviewed above did not find that survivors of childhood cancer demonstrated higher levels of depression when compared with the general population. In a more recent study, Kaplan, Busner, Weinhold, & Lenon (1987) assessed depressive symptomatology in child and adolescent oncology patients who were evaluated three times over the course of a year. The sample was composed of a variety of leukemic and nonleukemic patients, some of whom were in remission at the time of study while others were in relapse. Kaplan et al. (1987) found no differences between adolescent cancer patients' scores and a comparison adolescent sample from the general population on the *Beck Depression Inventory*. Using the *Children's Depression Inventory* with younger cancer patients they found that these children actually scored lower than the published norms reported for this instrument. The authors point out that these results are in contrast to studies of adult oncology patients in whom the prevalence of depression is over 20%. Particularly among adolescents, depressive symptoms were highly correlated with negative life events such as arguments with parents and restrictions on social activities and peer interactions. Interestingly, illness variables such as number of hospitalizations, relapse or remission status, and time since diagnosis did not predict depression scores among adolescents; however, depression in the child sample was related to total number of hospitalizations. The authors conclude that "psychosocial life events are an important source of variance of depressive symptoms in child and adolescent oncologic populations" (Kaplan et al., 1987, p. 787).

Overall, there is little evidence that chronically ill children are depressed. Kashani et al. (1981) found that among 100 preadolescent children admitted to a pediatric inpatient unit for treatment of a variety of medical problems depression was most consistently related to family history of depression and loss or absence of one parent from the home. The majority of these children had gastrointestinal disorders. Only 2 of the 7 children who met DSM-III diagnostic criteria for depression had a chronic illness, one with Friedreich's ataxia and the other with juvenile rheumatoid arthritis. None of the patients with leukemia or lymphoma was clinically depressed. The authors hypothesized that depression in the two patients with chronic illness may have been due to disease-related disruptions in the child's social interaction and mobility. In an effort to move beyond global characterizations of chronically ill children as depressed or nondepressed, and in order to develop appropriate psychosocial interventions for these children, future studies should focus on specific family factors, illness events (e.g. frequency of hospitalization, duration of treatment), and other stressful life events that may predispose some children to depressive or dysphoric symptomatology.

Stress and Coping with Chronic Illness

Koocher (1984) has suggested that the greatest psychological stressor facing individuals with chronic illness, particularly a life-threatening one, centers on the uncertainty regarding the duration of the illness and its outcome. Illness-related disruptions in normal developmental tasks and activities impose additional stressors on children and adolescents, but in spite of this many of these children adapt very well. Unfortunately, much of the empirical work in this area represents a search for psychopathology rather than focusing on how these children cope and what factors contribute to successful coping. At this point in time, we know very little about the coping strategies that chronically ill children use and what they understand about the coping process.

Moos and Tsu (1977) have developed a conceptual model which describes the coping tasks and strategies of individuals faced with the life crisis of physical illness. Seven major adaptive tasks are outlined: 1) dealing with pain and incapacitation; 2) dealing with the hospital environment and treatment procedures; 3) developing relationships with professional staff; 4) preserving emotional balance by managing feelings of anxiety, resentment, and isolation; 5) preserving a positive self-image; 6) preserving relationships with family and friends; and 7) preparing for an uncertain future.

Factors that affect the individual's perceptions of illness, his or her coping skills, and the outcome of these efforts include personal characteristics, environmental variables, and illness-related variables. Coping skills may involve denial or minimizing the seriousness of the situation, seeking relevant information, rehearsing possible outcomes, seeking emotional support from family, friends, and medical staff, mastering specific illness-related self-care tasks, setting concrete goals, and finding purpose or meaning in life events.

Wertlieb, Weigel, and Feldstein (1987) have employed a similar model to study how children cope with stressful experiences and, in particular, what problem-solving and emotion-management strategies they use. These investigators developed a methodology for assessing children's self-reports about their coping, what Wertlieb et al. (1987) refer to as "meta-coping." School-aged children's responses to questions about how they deal with stressful experiences in their lives were coded along dimensions which described the *focus* of coping behaviors (self, environment, or other), *function* (instrumental problem-solving behavior versus emotion-management coping behavior), and *mode* (information seeking, support seeking, direct action, inhibition of action, or intrapsychic). Using this scheme one can begin to examine the variety of coping strategies that children employ and the factors that affect the use of self- versus environment-directed modes of coping. For example, in preliminary analyses Wertlieb et al. (1987) found that girls reported proportionately more environment-focused coping behaviors (e.g. support seeking) than did boys, and self-reported use of emotion-management and intrapsychic strategies increased with age. This research offers a promising empirical approach toward understanding the coping behaviors of children in a variety of stress-inducing conditions, including those associated with chronic illness.

Stressful Life Events and Chronic Illness

While there is relatively little empirical data on the processes by which children cope with the stress of chronic illness, there has been some research examining the impact of psychological stress on health status and disease control in this population. Johnson (1986) reviewed this research in an earlier volume in this series. He concluded that the available empirical evidence supports the view that negative life changes and high levels of stress brought about by events such as parental loss, school failure, and problems with family and peer relationships may exacerbate physical symptoms in chronically ill children. Most of these findings come from studies of children with juvenile diabetes and cannot be readily generalized to other chronic conditions. Johnson (1986) reports that cumulative life events have been associated with a number of clinical measures of diabetes control such as blood sugar and urine ketone levels. It is not clear from the data currently available whether stress has a direct physiologic effect on diabetic control or if it acts indirectly by reducing therapeutic compliance, thereby disrupting health status.

Recently, Delamater and his colleagues (Delamater, Kurtz, Bubb, White, and Santiago, 1987; Delamater, Bubb et al., 1988) have examined the impact of psychological stress and coping on metabolic control among adolescents with type 1 diabetes. In one study (Delamater, Bubb et al., 1988), the effects of experimentally induced psychologic stress on specific physiologic measures were assessed. Subjects were divided into good, fair, and poor metabolic control groups on the basis of measures of *glycosylated hemoglobin* (Hb A1). During baseline and after each of 3, 10-minute stress conditions metabolic, hormonal, and cardiovascular measures were obtained. The stress conditions consisted of a cognitive quiz focusing on math and information questions, a mother-child interaction in which disagreements over the diabetes regimen were discussed, and a mother-child discussion on a more neutral topic. Findings indicated that metabolic control did not worsen immediately following an episode of acute psychological stress in good or poor control subjects; however, cardiovascular arousal increased, as did subjective perceptions of stress. Patients who began the study in poor metabolic control exhibited increased baseline diastolic blood pressure and heart rate, suggesting that adolescents in poor control may be at increased cardiovascular risk.

Given the difficulties in creating laboratory-induced stress of sufficient intensity to produce metabolic changes, Delamater, Bubb et al. (1988) suggest that more meaningful and ecologically valid studies of the relationship between psychological stress and metabolic control may derive from research on stress and coping in the patient's natural environment. In a related study, Delamater, Kurtz et al. (1987) found that adolescents in poor metabolic control employed more wishful thinking and avoidance/help-seeking modes of coping with a recent stressful event than did patients in good control. In describing a recent stressor, patients in good control primarily identified academic problems while those in poor control named diabetes-related difficulties most frequently. The frequency and severity of stress, as measured by the *Hassles Scale*, were not related to metabolic control. Delamater, Kurtz et al. (1987) conclude that the type of coping behavior used in managing stress, rather than the degree of stress, is related to metabolic control. They suggest that patients in poor control use inefficient coping strategies (e.g. hoping for a miracle, avoiding people).

In future research, studies should be extended to other chronic conditions in which specific physiological and clinical measures of disease control and health status can be examined in relation to specific stressful events, coping strategies, and behavioral compliance. In addition to coping and compliance, other factors that might mediate the relationship between stress and health status and perhaps buffer the individual against stressful life events, such as peer support and family cohesion (Walker & Greene, 1987), should also be studied. The relationship between family functioning and chronic childhood illness is considered in the next section.

FAMILY FUNCTIONING

The impact of chronic illness on the family has been discussed in a number of recent review articles (Burr, 1985; Drotar & Bush, 1985; Hamp, 1984; Johnson, 1985; Shapiro, 1983; Turk & Kerns, 1985; Van Dongen-Melman & Sanders-Woudstra, 1986). Psychosocial characteristics of the family, such as quality of interpersonal interactions and communication, levels of social support, and financial status, have been associated with both the health and emotional well-being of the chronically ill child (e.g., Anderson, Miller, Auslander, & Santiago, 1981; Daniels et al., 1987; Minuchin, Rosman, & Baker, 1978; Pless, Roghmann, & Haggerty, 1972; Waller et al., 1986; White, Kolman, Wexler, Polin, & Winter, 1984). Theoretical perspectives on family functioning now emphasize the transactional nature of interation among children, parents, and their environment; however, as the following discussion will demonstrate, empirical studies continue to focus primarily on unidirectional effects of family characteristics on the child or child effects on family. Given the breadth of this topic, the following review will be highly selective.

Sibling Adaptation

Ten years ago Lavigne and Ryan (1979) published a report describing increased psychologic maladjustment in siblings of chronically ill children. They studied 156 siblings of pediatric hematology, cardiology, and plastic surgery patients and compared them with siblings of healthy children on measures of emotional and behavioral functioning using the *Louisville Behavior Checklist*. It was hypothesized that various illnesses may affect siblings differentially as a function of specific disease characteristics such as its chronicity, severity, visibility, and degree of disruption in day-to-day family life. These investigators were also interested in whether the factors of sibling age and sex affected psychologic adjustment. It was found that siblings in the illness groups demonstrated more irritability and social withdrawal than healthy controls and this effect was strongest for siblings of children with visible handicaps such as cleft lip and palate (plastic surgery group). Significant sex × age interactions were obtained, with younger girls (3 to 6 years) demonstrating the same or higher levels of adjustment problems than younger boys, and older girls (7 to 13 years) showing the same or fewer problems than older boys. The latter finding contrasts with a report by Breslau, Weitzman, and Messenger (1981) in which younger male and older female siblings demonstrated more psychologic impairment. This discrepancy might be accounted for by the difference in studying sibling age versus sibling birth order. Lavigne and Ryan (1979) concluded that siblings of children with chronic illness are at increased risk for problems of behavioral and emotional adjustment.

There are methodological weaknesses in the Lavigne and Ryan (1979) study. Unfortunately, control and chronic illness siblings were not matched in terms of age and socioeconomic status, and parental education and income were higher in the healthy group, necessitating the use of covariance analyses. In addition, two siblings from each chronic illness family were recruited, thereby reducing independence of measures. However, this was one of the first large-scale studies of siblings of chronically ill children and, for the most part, these findings have stood the test of time.

More recent studies of siblings of chronically ill children support the view that these children are at mildly increased risk for psychosocial maladaptation, including increased aggression and delinquency (Breslau et al., 1981), withdrawal (Tritt & Esses, 1988), internalizing disorders (Cadman, Boyle, & Offord, 1988), and self-reported medical problems (Daniels, et al., 1986). Most researchers emphasize, however, that the majority of siblings of chronically ill children are psychologically healthy. Questions remain concerning the role of age, sex, disease severity/visibility, and family dynamics (Daniels et al., 1986; Drotar & Crawford, 1986) as mediators of psychosocial risk within this population. In an interesting adjunct to their study of siblings' psychologic functioning, Tritt and Esses (1988) conducted a semi-structured interview in which they asked siblings about their perceptions of the impact of chronic illness on the family. Siblings were highly sensitive to their parents' worries concerning the afflicted child. Many reported increased responsibilities and decreased attention as a result of having an ill sibling and this was accompanied by feelings of resentment. They often felt that the ill child received special treatment. Interestingly, Breslau et al. (1981) conducted a similar interview with mothers of chronically ill children. Most mothers denied that attention to siblings was affected by the presence of an ill child or that siblings resented their chronically ill brother or sister. Further studies aimed at understanding the transactional processes underlying family adaptation to the crisis of chronic illness would benefit not only from more refined measures of individual child and family functioning but also from measures that take into account family members' perceptions of illness impact and coping and, in particular, consistencies and discrepancies between parents and children on these dimensions.

Marital Functioning

In recent reviews it has been reported that marital distress, but not divorce, is more prevalent among parents of chronically ill children (Johnson, 1985; Sabbeth & Leventhal, 1984). At least one study (Koocher & O'Malley, 1981) found that parents of chronically ill children reported that the illness brought them closer together as a couple and as parents. In a critique of the literature, Sabbeth and Leventhal (1984) note that most studies examining this issue have failed to employ adequate control groups and, by their cross-sectional design, have not been able to examine changes in marital functioning over the course of the illness. Studies examining marital harmony versus distress have used widely differing methods of assessment and often poorly defined criterion measures. To increase our understanding of why these parents who are experiencing more marital distress do not seem to divorce more, and how marital distress impacts on the psychosocial functioning of the chronically ill child, Sabbeth and Leventhal (1984) suggest that future studies should explore the potentially adaptive function of conflict and should examine more specific aspects of marital adjustment, such as communication, decision making, problem solving, and role flexibility.

Family Characteristics Affecting Child Functioning

Johnson (1985) has pointed out that parenting the chronically ill child involves at least three major tasks or goals: 1) managing the illness and helping the child to assume this responsibility; 2) assisting the child in coping with illness while encouraging normal development; and 3) normalizing family functioning while dealing with the disruptions in lifestyle brought on by the presence of a chronically ill family member. Psychological adjustment and disease control in chronically ill children have been associated with specific family interactional patterns which are not unlike those deemed to be important to the psychological well-being of healthy children. It has been suggested that excessive parental restriction, anxiety, overprotectiveness, high levels of conflict and disordered modes of communication, and limited resources and social supports will lead to psychologic maladaptation (see reviews by Burr, 1985; Johnson, 1985). However, there is no uniform pattern of pathology within dysfunctional families of chronically ill children. Much of the literature in this area is based on clinical observation and theorizing, or on studies which lack methodological rigor. Some recent empirical reports that illustrate how family characteristics may relate to the health and psychologic functioning of the ill child are described below.

Waller et al. (1986) examined specific family support behaviors in relation to metabolic control in 42 children and adolescents with diabetes mellitus. Child as well as parent perceptions of family behavior were obtained using a scale designed specifically to assess psychosocial functioning in families with a diabetic child. Three dimensions of family support were derived from this scale: warmth/caring, guidance/control, and problem solving. Glycosylated hemoglobin served as the criterion measure. Recent glycemic control was significantly correlated with three individual items from the family behavior scale: 1) whether the parent watches while the child tests for sugar, 2) whether the parents write down the sugar tests, and 3) whether the child has someone in the family to talk to about diabetes. The family support dimension of guidance/control was significantly correlated with metabolic control, as was the dimension of warmth/caring, although the latter relationship obtained only for girls. Problem solving was not related to metabolic control. Some interesting age effects were found such that increased family guidance/control was associated with better metabolic control for younger children (less than 13 years) as opposed to adolescents. Younger children who reported that they frequently tested their own sugars and took care of their diabetes themselves were in poorer control. For adolescents, on the other hand, more self-care responsibility by the teen-ager, but with continued involvement by the parents, such as parent watching while the child tests for sugar, was associated with better metabolic control. This study, then, points to some specific family behaviors that correlate with at least one measure of health status in diabetic children.

Daniels et al. (1987) studied the relationship between family functioning and psychological adjustment in 93 patients with juvenile rheumatic disease (RD). These children were compared to healthy siblings and matched controls. Measures included maternal reports of child behavior and adjustment problems, parental functioning (depression and physical symptoms), family stressors (number of negative life events, sibling functioning, and parental report of burden of illness on the family), and family resources (Cohesion, Expressiveness, and Conflict subscales of the Family Environment Scale). Findings indicated that mother and father dysfunction, sibling dysfunction, stressful life events, and burden of illness on the family predicted adjustment problems in the RD sample. Adjustment problems in their siblings were predicted by low levels of family cohesion and expressiveness. Stronger relationships between maternal functioning and child adjustment obtained for the RD patients and their siblings than for healthy controls. Mothers in the RD group reported significantly more depression. It was also found that parental dysfunction was associated with more physical problems in the RD patients such as arthritic pain and morning stiffness.

In sum, the findings from this correlational study demonstrate that risk of psychosocial and physical problems in a population of chronically ill children and their siblings is increased significantly by the presence of specific family factors, most notably parental dysfunction, stressful life events, and burden of illness on the family. Longitudinal research is needed to examine the direction of effects with respect to these findings. The finding that family interactional patterns, such as cohesion and expressiveness, were more important in the adjustment of healthy siblings and controls than for RD patients warrants further study. It may be that individuals' sensitivity to these aspects of family functioning varies in relation to the severity of illness (Daniels et al., 1987).

Daniels et al.'s (1987) result of significantly more depression in the mothers of RD patients is consistent with other reports of increased maternal mental health problems in families of chronically ill children. Mothers typically bear the burden of responsibility for the day-to-day care of the chronically ill child. This undoubtedly places greater personal strain and psychological distress on these mothers than is typically experienced by mothers of healthy children (Johnson, 1985). Jessop, Riessman, and Stein (1988) examined maternal adjustment in mothers of 209 children with diverse chronic conditions. The *Psychiatric Symptom Index* was used to assess maternal mental health and, in particular, symptom patterns of anxiety and depression, anger/hostility, and somatization. Results revealed that a medical provider's estimate of the extent of burden of the child's medical condition bore no relation to maternal psychological status, however maternal report of the child's functional status was significantly related to the presence of psychiatric symptomatology in the mother. The more severe the child's morbidity status, as perceived by the mother, the poorer was her mental health. Demographic and descriptive characteristics, such as parental education, family income and employment, and age and sex of the child did not predict maternal psychiatric symptomatology. In regression analyses maternal psychiatric symptoms were predicted by maternal physical health, impact of illness on the family, the presence of other life stressors, and whether the mother had someone to talk to about her problems. These factors mediated the relationship between child functional status and maternal mental health and point to the need for multivariate models to describe risk in this population. Jessop et al. (1988) conclude that:

> even a seemingly objective stressor like chronic illness in childhood cannot be fully understood apart from the larger context in which this event is embedded. A particularly significant aspect of this context is the impact that the illness has on the family, the meaning of the illness, the disruption it brings in its stead, and the resources that can be brought to bear to deal with it. Also significant are co-existing stressors and health problems in mothers and other family members. (p. 154)

SUMMARY

Research examining the impact of chronic illness on the child's cognitive and social-emotional functioning, as well as it's impact on the family, has been reviewed in this chapter. Overall, the available empirical data suggest that most children with chronic illness do not manifest intellectual impairments or psychological disturbance and there is no "personality type" that characterizes this child population. As a group, these children do not demonstrate elevated levels of depression or lowered self-esteem. Similarly, the families of chronically ill children, on the whole, are functioning well and demonstrate remarkable resiliency. Chronic childhood illness does pose increased risk, however, for subtle neuropsychological deficits and behavioral and adjustment problems. Estimates of risk vary as a function of population and measurement characteristics. An effort has been made in this chapter to identify specific organismic and environmental correlates of both psychosocial maladaptation and coping.

The severity of disease does not consistently relate to the presence of adjustment problems; however, the level of functional disability in the child is predictive. Cognitive deficits are highly disease-specific and may occur as direct manifestations of CNS injury or secondary to therapeutic interventions such as the use of medications or irradiation. There is modest evidence that life stress can exacerbate disease-related physical symptomatology, although it is not clear whether stress has a direct effect on physiologic functioning or if it acts indirectly by reducing adherence to therapy which, in turn, compromises health status.

Because most research has focused on identifying psychopathology or dysfunction there is to date very little information concerning clinically ill children's coping styles, their understanding of coping processes ("meta-coping"), or the factors which contribute to successful coping in this population. In addition, children's perceptions of the chronic illness experience and its effects on their lives and their families have not been well studied.

In terms of family functioning, recent research suggests that both siblings and mothers of chronically ill children exhibit increased levels of psychologic distress and maladaptation. Marital disharmony but not divorce is more common in these families. Specific family interaction patterns, such as overprotection and high levels of conflict, as well as parental psychologic dysfunction, have been associated with child adjustment problems.

Further research using multivariate, transactional models is needed to examine specific factors in the child, parent, and environment that impact on psychosocial functioning and adaptation to chronic illness. Child variables should include assessment of premorbid personality and behavioral functioning, severity of illness and level of functional disability, and both subjective and objective measures of stress and coping. Family interaction patterns deemed to be important to the psychological well-being of healthy children, such as cohesion, communication, and independence-fostering, apply as well to chronically ill children. More refined and psychometrically sound measures of these dimensions of family functioning are needed. Finally, the broader environmental context and, in particular, the availability of social and educational supports for these children and their families requires further study. Efforts to identify simple relationships between childhood chronic illness and psychological adaptation have been unsuccessful. Moderating variables that exacerbate (e.g., parental dysfunction) or ameliorate (e.g., social support) the effects of chronic illness must be considered in any model of psychosocial functioning in this population.

5

CLINICAL INTERVENTION

PROFESSIONAL ATTENTION TO CHRONIC ILLNESS

A review of the relatively recent development of a professional perspective on the chronically ill child in several key health care disciplines will be instructive. For example, let us first consider pediatric medicine and the place of chronically ill children in its recent history. As we noted in Chapter 2, technological breakthroughs in the prevention of infectious childhood diseases during this century have led to major shifts in the nature and focus of pediatric health care. A strong humanistic orientation within pediatrics, along with projected surpluses in trained pediatricians during the next 20 years, have begun to alter the original focus of pediatric medicine from primarily an acute intervention mode in service delivery to one that emphasizes disease prevention, treatment of mishaps and accidental injuries, and an expanded purview which includes efforts to minimize psychosocial morbidity in children and adolescents (Cohen, 1984). Further, the primary-care pediatric health care provider is gradually being shaped, through federal and academic influences, to pay greater attention to the promotion of physical and psychological *wellness* in children and adolescents through increased health education, alteration of lifestyle factors, and through the early identification of psychosocial and developmental problems. Attention to the quality of life and multiple needs of the chronically ill child and his family has increased concomitant with these currents within pediatric practice (Green, 1983). It is not very clear, however, how pediatric providers will actually increase or improve their services. Now, as in the past, pediatricians attend to the medical needs of the chronically ill and we do know that these providers also offer supportive counseling in many cases. Whether or not this form of counseling is guided by a particular intervention philosophy is dependent upon the orientation and training of the practitioner. Pediatric providers have also been active in nontraditional outreach and patient education activities such as disease-related camping experiences and public forums on childhood chronic illnesses. While pediatricians have long been thought of as advocates and case managers for chronically ill children, the time and labor involved in such cases can be tremendous. Thus, it is likely that pediatric providers have real limits to how involved they can become with the multiple problems of the chronically ill child.

The inclusion of chronically ill groups as a funding priority within health-oriented federal and private foundations, and the growing number of studies and editorial articles appearing in the pediatric literature, all serve as tangible evidence of a mounting concern about the needs of these children within primary and subspecialty pediatric medicine. It is clear, however, that many gaps remain in the health care systems designed to serve the chronically ill child (Stein, Jessop & Riessman, 1983) which appear to be consistent across all or most of the various disease types. The intentions of this burgeoning movement are quite good but implementation will be ill-fated if there is a dearth of empirically tested methods, fiscally responsible reimbursement schemes, and a broadly based commitment to this area at the level of medical training and research program funding.

Although American medicine has traditionally been almost exclusively focused upon the concept of effectiveness of cure and treatment, and for good reason, the focus of the nursing and medical social work professions, perhaps by virtue of their day-to-day tasks, has been primarily on improving the overall quality of care to the patient through in-hospital and post-discharge social support. Since nurses have consistently been on the front line of health care for acutely and chronically ill children it should be no surprise that much of the earliest and more clinically oriented writings about the familial and psychological aspects of chronically ill children and adults can be found in their professional literature. Nurses have long been interested in finding ways to address and ameliorate those behavioral, psychological and social problems which impact on the child patients' and their parents' ability to cope with disease-onset, to tolerate stressful procedures, and successfully negotiate the hospitalization experience (Lewandowski, 1984; Horner, 1987; Hunsberger, Love & Byrne, 1984; Seahill, 1969; Wu, 1965). However, the nursing profession's evolution has only recently led to a greater emphasis on clinical theory wedded to careful empirical research, the dominant perspective in our current conceptualization of science, and so their contribution has been largely viewed as qualitative, anecdotal and, therefore, suspected of being inordinately biased. Similarly, research emanating from the medical social work profession has been largely qualitative in nature. This has changed dramatically in recent years with the emergence of several important theoretical and empirical analyses of the relationship among familial and social-contextual factors and physical conditions in the chronically ill.

Child psychiatric medicine also has a documented history of attention to chronically ill children, although it has been of a rather limited nature. This history begins substantially in the 1940s, although a few earlier reports do exist. These initial case studies were primarily concerned with the effects of hospitalization and illness on parent-child relations and the possible emotional trauma that may be caused. Somewhat tangentially related are Rene Spitz's (1946) classic papers identifying the phenomenon of hospitalism in infants and very young children. His case descriptions were especially dramatic examples of the potentially powerful psychological and behavioral effects that medical interventions could exert on the development and emotional well-being of the child. Spitz's work has been used widely to bolster arguments in favor of psychologically sensitive and humane interventions for hospitalized children, although the conditions of care in American hospitals and adoptive nurseries have improved rather dramatically since the period during which his observations were made.

Consider Hobbs et al.'s (1985) description of psychiatric attention to chronically ill children during subsequent years:

> In the late 1950's and early 1960's, there began to appear articles and book chapters concerning the special needs of dying children and their families and the proper response to them by physicians and nurses. Shortly thereafter began the appearance of articles focused on mental health issues generally applicable to the care of children with chronic illnesses and their parents. To a large extent, these articles were again based on case studies and thoughtful impressions of clinicians who looked at their material through psychoanalytically-oriented theories rather than data systematically collected with more objective measures. Partly as a result of their theoretical bias, these authors tended to focus on the more negative outcomes and processes inherent in chronic illness and hospitalization. (p. 57)

Breslau (1985) has summarized a more recent and gradual shift in perspective within the child psychiatric approach from one that primarily emphasizes a psychopathological view to the more current, uncertain stance. She points out that carefully controlled studies reported in the late seventies and early eighties suggest that we were not able to accurately predict psychopathology for individual cases nor across groups of children within various disease types. In more specialized referral settings, however, the rates of diagnosable disorder can be found to be somewhat higher. Consider Rait, Jacobsen, Lederberg, and Holland's (1988) summary following a review of 58 pediatric cancer patients seen through a psychiatric consultation service:

> The most prevalent diagnosis was adjustment disorder, which is similar to findings with adult cancer patients. In a parallel review of psychiatric consultations with adult cancer patients . . . 64% received the diagnosis of adjustment disorder. At the same time, (it was) concluded that DSM-III is not well suited to describing the range of individual responses to medical illness but that adjustment disorder best describes reactions of these patients in the present classification system. This conclusion also extends to our experience with pediatric cancer patients. . . . In all likelihood, the accurate psychiatric diagnosis of children with cancer will depend on general diagnostic advances in child psychopathology. (p. 364)

For now it should suffice to say that some controversy and confusion characterizes the applicability of psychiatric nosologies and models of treatment to chronic illness (Pless & Zvagulis, 1981), but how much this uncertainty has influenced actual child psychiatric practice patterns with chronically ill children is not known. And, as in the case of pediatric physicians, it does not appear that an articulated philosophy or model of treatment has been sufficiently developed within child psychiatry that allows it to specify its potential contribution, or the applicability and efficacy of its methods and general approach (Jellinek, 1982). Despite Rait et al.'s (1988) feeling that DSM-III is not adequate for classifying psychological and psychiatric responses to medical illness, it is used widely for just this purpose. Imposition of a mental disorder model with such children, even through use of the relatively non-specific *adjustment disorder* classification may have little benefit in both assessment and treatment planning and can carry along with it some very distinct disadvantages.

Emphasis on the chronically ill child within developmental and clinical psychology has also been derived from a rather gradual process that has been affected by many of the same factors we have noted previously.

Child development experts have written about the ramifications of illness and injury on the growing child for many years and we have reviewed this in Chapter 3. Those psychologists concerned with family influences on the child have helped to focus research and practice on the importance of this variable in adjustment to various stress-related conditions and trauma, including chronic and acute illnesses (Shapiro, 1983). Psychologists have also attempted to contribute to the study of the chronically ill child through application of personality and adaptational theories to this group, through a recognition of the inappropriateness of a pathology model to explain elevated emotional distress as a response to illness (Drotar & Bush, 1985), and ongoing attempts to apply therapeutic models and techniques to the chronically ill child and her family (Routh, 1988). Much of our review in this volume is based upon the more empirical child health psychology research literature conducted during the past 20 years.

An additional development during the past two decades that reinforces the sense that child psychological researchers and practitioners are becoming more formally committed to the chronically ill child is the Pediatric Psychology movement within professional child psychology in the United States and abroad (Routh, 1988; Roberts, 1986). This trend has been driven by broader expansion of clinical psychology into health care contexts and by pediatric physicians' willingness to collaborate with psychologists in the treatment of an array of common childhood problems. Indeed, a pediatric or child health subspecialization arising from within developmental and child-clinical psychology promises to spawn new generations of professionals specifically interested in applications of psychological theory and practice to the special nature and needs of the pediatric patient, including the chronically ill. This subspecialty group, distinct from behavioral medicine in its attempt to expand its purview to include systemic, cognitive, and psychodynamic processes, promises to emerge as a major force in both research and treatment in child health.

MODELS AND MEASURES

We have made the point repeatedly in this book that children who are affected by chronic illness, as a group, do not go on to manifest moderate to serious psychological symptomatology which would meet more conservative criteria for a psychiatric disorder. And we have pointed out that models of evaluation and treatment that use a psychopathology orientation can be fated to be inadequate and even inappropriate in clinical work with children and families. Still, this overall view must be tempered by some facts that emerge from the research and clinical experience reported to date. First of all, it does appear that statistical risk likelihoods for psychological and psychiatric symptomatology are higher in samples of chronically ill children as compared with both matched controls from the heterogeneous population and unaffected sibling controls. Estimates range from 1.5 to 3 times greater risk for chronically ill children (Pless, 1984). Further, most of the children who might benefit from mental health services probably do not receive them, through an array of factors including self-selection, lack of referral by medical providers who may have difficulty distinguishing transient adjustment reactions from more serious symptoms, insufficient resources, and nonavailability of specialized services (Pless, Satterwhite & VanVechten, 1978). And, the parents of these children have been reported to frequently indicate a perceived need for supportive mental health counseling even when their primary health care provider has judged this to be unnecessary and/or has failed to refer (Stein, Jessop & Riessman, 1983).

It is also important to note that more recent empirical studies have applied stricter definitions of disorder to classify psychological and psychiatric outcomes in this subgroup. If one were to employ more liberal criteria for psychological dysfunction, then the prevalence rates could rise dramatically. For example, if we expanded our case definition to include more common cases of transient and/or recurrent crisis periods characterized by relatively intense psychological, behavioral, or social difficulties then many more children would be included in the group eligible for psychosocial interventions. Also, if we went even further to include maladaptive behaviors that interfere with *optimum* adjustment to a particular disease regimen, or even those that detract from the provider-patient interaction, then greater numbers of children who are chronically ill, and their families, would be candidates for mental health related intervention.

Therefore, it appears that the standard of psychological health one employs will largely determine the resulting prevalence estimates for undesired psychological and social outcomes in children affected by a chronic illness. If our model of psychological health is more strictly defined via the level of functional status residing somewhere within the broad normal range, then most chronically ill children will be characterized as such. However, if one applies a model that emphasizes optimum quality of life and full realization of individual potential, then chronic illness represents a persistent and powerful source of adversity that can significantly threaten both of these goals in a child's life. Indeed, more clinically based case reports of chronically ill children, despite their known methodologic limitations, have tended to paint a more pessimistic picture in terms of the psychological health and overall adjustment of chronically ill children (Drotar & Bush, 1985). And some could argue that such psychologically in-depth studies may have a certain advantage in detecting more subtle but clinically pertinent problems which behavioral checklists, personality inventories, and psychiatric nosologies cannot possibly capture or convey.

In view of these factors, clinical attempts to prevent such problems, equip the child and family with adequate coping skills, and develop effective treatments for moderate to serious psychological symptoms, become very relevant. We do know that maladjustment to varying degrees and at acutely stressful times during the childhood years can characterize the chronically ill child's psychological profile. Such maladjustment can be transient or persistent, adaptive or destructive. In any case, it is important to closely consider the full range of assessment and intervention that have been proposed and studied in the health and psychological literatures as they apply to both psychologically disordered children and the larger sub-clinical group who are at risk or compromised in some meaningful way. These techniques and approaches are a rather broad collection emanating from major treatment orientations to be found in the backdrop provided by more traditional child mental health research and practice. Although we are beginning to see more techniques specifically developed for application to the chronically ill child and adolescent population, these remain in the minority.

We have already noted that many clinical methods have largely been based on available models of psychopathology or life stress adaptation primarily derived from adult and family samples. Child models sensitive to self-perceptual and developmental factors are sorely lacking. While the field appears cognizant of and quite sensitive to these factors in its thinking about childhood chronic illness, it is not at all apparent that we have been able to incorporate this heightened awareness into our evaluation and treatment approaches. And, it is our view that much of this criticism can also be levied on the larger child mental health field which has provided the foundation for many techniques used within this group of children and families. In fact, it is possible that work with chronically ill children, by virtue of being directed toward increased attention to the fuller range of psychological coping, will develop new and more sensitive measures as compared to methods found in pathology oriented clinical research and practice.

From a practical perspective, however, existing models and measures, whether they take an adaptational, psychopathologic, individualistic, or systemic orientation, probably have much to contribute in practice. For example, it is likely that some responses to the stressors of chronic illness are adequately explained by models of mental health etiology or through use of measures keyed to psychopathology, especially in more dramatic and severe reactions. It is a recurrent finding in the literature that preexisting child and familial characteristics or dysfunction can mediate psychological outcomes in affected children and their families. Adaptational models and their derivative methods are useful for explaining more situationally or disease-specific reactions to chronic illness, and they allow us to study the continuum of negative through positive coping within chronic illness and its associated adversity. But it is clear in the case of clinical work with children and families that all of these major theoretical orientations to chronic illness need to evolve further into more developmentally and contextually sensitive models.

ASSESSMENT APPROACHES

As the three previous chapters have suggested, there is a wide array of child, family, disease, and environmental factors that need to be assessed prior to any conclusions regarding the need for clinical intervention or what form necessary interventions should take. Assessment procedures need to be fashioned in such a way so as to be comprehensive enough to address these potential influences. The specific measures used and the general context for assessment need to be considered carefully as well. It is our view that the initial focus of psychosocial evaluation of the chronically ill child and family should be on the assessment of impact on the measurable aspects of child and familial functional status and the overall quality of life. At this point a nonspecific, *disease-global* model of illness and coping can be useful. Part of this evaluation will certainly address psychological and emotional upset which can diminish functioning and quality of life or represent a risk to future health status. However, clinical intervention, when warranted, is most likely to be effective when it can be relevant to improvement of functional status through an understanding of the effects on the child and family as individuals and within a system. This understanding is achieved through both objective assessments by the clinician and more subjective appraisals by the affected child and family. At the next level of assessment, however, the disease-specific features need to be considered along with those factors that are generalizable across illness types to derive a more complete assessment for the individual case. As a result of this process, several important clinical questions should be posed.

In performing a clinical assessment of a child with a chronic physical illness, there are six major questions that should be addressed. Two questions concern the illness and its physical effects on the child, two concern the developmental and psychosocial effects on the child, and two concern the effects on the family. These questions are: *What is the extent of the disease and its complications in the child?*, *What are the physical effects of the illness on the child?*, *How has the illness affected the child's performance at home, with peers, and at school?*, *How has the child adjusted to the illness?*, *What impact does the child's illness have on the family and its members?*, *How has the family adjusted to the special impact or burden of the illness?* (Leventhal, 1984, pp.71-72) (emphasis in original)

These questions are never simple to answer as they require time to explore, and the answers can fluctuate as the course of a particular disease and its treatment proceeds. And there is some evidence to suggest that most psychosocial interventions related to chronic illness in childhood are often limited to shorter-term consultations and/or time-limited treatments (Jay & Wright, 1985). However, the minimal goals of an initial evaluation should be an estimation of changes in functioning as compared with previous status, a determination of major strengths and weaknesses in the affected child and family which might enhance or diminish coping, and the identification of specific goals for intervention or case monitoring which will be pursued in a planful manner.

The methods employed to achieve these ends are varied and, as we have mentioned previously, most have been directly derived from the existing child and family mental health armamentarium. Achievement and intelligence tests, symptom inventories, self-report questionnaires, observational schemes, play techniques, structured and semi-structured clinical interviews, and an array of projective techniques have all been used with the chronically ill child or adolescent. As we noted previously, early studies examined the personality characteristics of chronically ill children almost exclusively. More recently a greater emphasis has been placed on cognitive/neuropsychological and self-perceptual (e.g., self-esteem and self-concept) measures within this literature. One suspects that in practice, given the confines of many medical settings where these children are primarily seen, the approach to psychosocial evaluation may be far less structured and formalized than in research applications. Psychological and psychiatric assessments, in actuality, may often render rather rapidly conceived clinical assessments based on relatively short interviews in combination with the clinician's accrued experience, the immediate pattern of presenting symptoms, and a variety of situationally salient features. However, regular use of structured objective psychological measures promises to more fully inform the clinical process. The psychometric properties and external validities of some of these measures, however, remain somewhat uncertain, especially as they pertain to chronically ill children. This situation will hopefully be improved through more clinical research with such children.

There is also a small but growing number of measures that have been developed for application to specific chronic disease types. Commonly, these measures are paper-and-pencil questionnaires or structured interviews which tap the child or parents' attitudes, knowledge, behaviors, and decision making relevant to a certain disease and its medical regimen. Although there are problems associated with using self-reports in psychological and behavioral assessments, such a measurement approach holds special promise for learning more specific information about the child or parent's behaviors and attitudinal stance associated with a particular disease. These measures have been used in conjunction with studies of compliance, disease-related knowledge, preparation for stressful medical procedures, and anxiety or pain reduction. Early examples of such measures would include the McGill Pain Questionnaire (Melzack, 1975), the Asthmatic Potential Scale (Block, Jennings, Harvey, & Simpson, 1964), the Family Functioning Index (Pless & Satterwhite, 1973), and the Asthma Symptom Checklist (Kinsman, O'Banion, Resnikoff, Luparello, & Spector, 1973). More recent examples would include the Medical Compliance Incomplete Stories Test (Czajkowski & Koocher, 1987), the Diabetes Opinion Survey (Johnson, 1988), and others.

However, the studies to date suggest that the relationships between these self-reported variables and actual physical or behavioral outcomes are not at all simple or direct (Johnson, 1988). For example, in diabetes mellitus assessments of subjectively reported knowledge, attitudes and behaviors by children and families do not automatically translate into good versus poor clinical outcomes, such as consistent metabolic control or behavioral adherence to the medical regimen. And, since most measures have been used only by their creators and perhaps a handful of collaborators, most cannot claim independent replication or substantiation. Also, few measures offer adequate norms due to difficulties associated with pooling sufficiently large standardization samples, the immense variation in the physical status of children affected with the same disease or chronic condition, and relatively low clinical demand across many primary- or secondary-level health care settings. Most of the available disease-specific measures pertain to more discrete and/or prevalent disorders such as diabetes mellitus, cystic fibrosis, and the childhood cancers. Attempts to develop broader measures of functioning for the chronically ill in general, and children in particular, have been somewhat sporadic and infrequent.

There is an emerging consensus in this field, as in child mental health, that measurement of only one or two aspects of individual or familial functioning in isolation will necessarily limit the clinician's understanding of the multiplicity of processes involved in psychological coping with chronic disease and the manifestation of reactive disorders. However, the required multidimensional assessments are often time consuming and not practical in many clinical settings. They may even constitute an excessive or overly invasive level of evaluation when one considers the good probability that significant disorder will not be encountered in the majority of chronically ill children. Decisions about the breadth and type of evaluation need to be tempered by the many points we have already tried to make in this book, and they will also need to be continually modified by pragmatic concerns.

Some assessment approaches, such as those with a more strictly behavioral orientation, may not require such breadth in assessment since their purview is confined to more operationally defined factors through a functional analysis of behavior emphasizing specific behaviors targeted for change, the relevant environmental contingencies, and the necessary reinforcement schedules for instituting change. Measures within such an approach include personal diaries or structured schedules through which patients keep record of self-administered medical procedures or disease-related behaviors, such as dietary intake or exercise. In a similar vein, family-systemic approaches which do not preoccupy themselves unduly with concepts and notions about individual psychopathology or personality characteristics also tend to require less intensive psychometric evaluation of *all* components, often choosing to use observable relationships among family members or clinical estimates of familial coping style as the focus for both evaluation and eventual treatment.

No matter which clinical approach is taken, symptoms of maladjustment associated with chronic illness need to be placed in the context in which they have occurred. Those symptoms that can be wholly or primarily attributed to disease-specific events or conditions need to be distinguished from those that have a longer history in the child or family. The clinician needs to be aware that the chronically ill child and his family, like other clients, will often arrive at times of crisis. Such crises can be self-defined, or may be determined by their health care providers. These crises can represent reasonable responses to dramatic or sudden changes in medical status as well as overreactions on the part of parents or health providers. Reports of acute depression, anxiety, hostility, social withdrawal, and other symptoms will accompany these children and their parents who are often referred soon after a medical diagnosis has been made, or if a serious relapse has occurred, a medical treatment has not been successful, or when medical provider-patient relations have become inordinately strained. Mental status at these times, both actual and as reported by others, needs to be compared and contrasted with more common and prototypical patterns of psychological and behavioral functioning in the child and family. And, at times, the focus of intervention and education will need to be the health care providers themselves and not the affected child or family.

INTERVENTION TECHNIQUES

Pediatric medicine, child health psychology, and psychiatric intervention research have focused on several overlapping aspects or clinical issues of chronic illness during childhood. Johnson (1988) has outlined these to include the *management of illness*, which entails variables such as disease-relevant knowledge, attitudes, skills, and medical regimen adherence. A second major approach has focused on *child coping with disease*, which includes assessment and treatment of psychological upset, stress resistance and vulnerability, and procedure-specific psychological responses. A third major focus has been *family effects*, including the impact on parental mental health and coping, sibling outcomes, and consequences relevant to altered family relationships. We would hasten to add that these approaches need to be contrasted across at least three predominant health care service delivery modes, namely, the *prevention* mode (health education and preparation for anticipated symptoms or procedures), the *intervention* mode (treatment after significant problems develop), and the *case monitoring* mode (follow-up programs for children defined at risk). Within the resulting matrix of approaches for examining clinical interventions, some techniques exist which merit special mention and brief description in this chapter.

One major approach is reflected in a collection of more broadly defined studies of child and family coping with disease onset and the maintenance of coping during the disease's subsequent course.

This approach has been somewhat generic and attempts to cross the boundaries between various chronic illnesses and conditions to identify common principles for explaining good versus poor adjustment to disease. The presumed goal of these theoretical and empirical studies is to provide guidance to *all* efforts to improve the psychosocial status of affected children, primarily by identifying positive coping strategies used by all affected children showing successful adjustment. Also, the special case of chronic illness during childhood has been thought to contain valuable lessons about human psychological adjustment in the face of other types of stressful life conditions. The approach has been influenced theoretically and methodologically by broad models of stress and coping such as those proposed by Lazarus and Launier (1978), which include emphasis on several aspects of psychological adaptation including behavioral, cognitive, emotional, and social processes. Studies using this general approach have considered the differences in the child's subjective perceptions about the significance or impact of their disease (Yamamoto, 1979), or have described the range of behavioral strategies the child may employ to counteract impairment caused by a particular disease (Drotar & Bush, 1985; Spinetta & Maloney, 1978; and Zeitlin, 1980). Other examples include studies that look at cognitive efforts to learn about a disease, or to buffer the child through the use of directed fantasy, autosuggestion, and hypnotherapeutic techniques.

The research designs of these studies tend to draw samples from good versus poor adjustment groups for direct comparison. Many have strongly emphasized the family context and the role of parental modelling in the child's poor versus good adjustment to disease. *Stress resil-*

ience, vulnerability and *protective factors* are keywords in this literature. In a related vein, some clinical investigators have examined the child and familial capacities for coping with more broadly defined life stress in the hope that these abilities have direct relevance not only to the child's adjustment to disease but also to the minimization or maximization of stress's effects on functional status (see also J. Johnson, 1986). Examples include studies by Bedell et al. (1977), Chase & Jackson (1981), Grant, Kyle, Teichman, & Mendeles (1974), and Smith, Gad, & O'Grady (1983). They combine to suggest that an array of coping styles do exist across affected individuals and their families, and that knowledge of these styles can inform therapeutic and educational approaches.

Other general approaches have focused on primary prevention of more serious psychological and family problems through prophylactic support or health education. Some researchers and clinicians have suggested that most clinical efforts, especially at the primary care level of service delivery, should be proactive and largely educational (Drotar & Bush, 1985). Indeed, many health care providers are engaged in this type of activity within the primary and secondary medical service delivery systems. However, attention to patient education is highly variable across such health care settings and even across different providers found within the same health setting. From a cost efficiency point of view this approach seems as though it might be the most effective, but this has not been demonstrated empirically. It is likely that the same logistical factors known to constrain the provision of mental health services in primary care settings would also act to reduce efforts in preventive intervention for chronic illnesses or conditions.

It is clear that preventive efforts can take many forms. One-to-one health education and problem solving, home visits, disease-specific summer camps, peer and parental support groups, and even social skills training have been employed. Most clinical outcome studies, at least those which have been published to date, have been able to claim improved clinical outcome in chronically ill children and their parents, as compared with those children who did not receive such prevention services. It is likely that this form of health care delivery will be the predominant vehicle for psychosocial services for most affected children and families during the decades ahead.

A third set of studies has examined intervention for psychiatric or psychologic problems after psychological problems have developed. Approaches to ameliorate psychological and/or family problems associated with chronic illness in children have ranged from individual psychodynamic or cognitive-behavioral therapy to group counseling, auto-suggestion and hypnotherapy, relaxation therapy, and other specific behavioral techniques. There is clearly an overlap of the methods used in this approach and the first group of studies described previously. However, the studies differ typically in their more narrow focus on identified psychiatric or psychological disorders subsequent to disease onset, most often child or family behavioral patterns, such as op-positionality and interactional conflict, generalized and specific patterns of elevated anxiety and/or depressive symptoms, increased social with-drawal or isolation, sibling and peer difficulties, and the negative effects on work or school performance. More generic child and family therapy or counseling has also been a common focus within studies using this approach, with a number of outcome studies claiming to effect desired change in both the affected children and their families.

> Psychotherapy oriented toward managing the emotional trauma of cancer assists the patient in accepting the disease and in confronting its personal significance. Basic emotional factors that must be considered when work-ing with cancer patients include isolation, pain, loss of control, despair, fear of death, family dynamics, and religious dilemmas ... the central aim of therapy is to increase emotional communication and assist in replacing denial and emotional distance with openness and participation. (Feinstein, 1983, p. 2)

Applications of more traditional, individual psychotherapy with child cancer patients are not easily found in the recent empirical literature. And yet, we suspect this may be a predominant treatment strategy with many chronically ill children who are referred to child mental health generalists currently in practice in the United States. We must pause to wonder whether existing mental health treatment orientations represent suitable models for clinical intervention with the chronically ill, just as there is some question that existing psychiatric nosologies leave much to be desired within this subgroup of children. In the absence of a well formulated theoretical model which can guide therapeutic efforts, we cannot fault practitioners for relying on their general treatment strate-gies.

In the clinical research literature it is more common to find examples of specialized therapeutic approaches focused on stress management, behavioral pain control, and the engendering of positive coping strate-gies through directive counseling and health education. It is likely that less operationalized therapeutic methods do not lend themselves easily to empirical inquiries and, therefore, are not equally represented in the professional literature. One exception to this is the application of play techniques or play therapy that has been reported in more clinically oriented psychological, social work, and nursing literatures (Petrillo & Sanger, 1972; Crocker, 1978; Freud, 1952; Hardgrove, 1977). Ongoing issues in empirically based child psychology research concerning the therapeutic efficacy of play therapy, however, will probably continue to seriously limit its application within mainstream clinical research studies (Milos & Reis, 1982). Play techniques as a clinical intervention with younger children who are medically ill, however, are used widely and appear extremely popular in medical settings (Peterson and Ridley-Johnson, 1980). This will probably remain the case despite a rather serious lack of adequate cross-validational and treatment outcome studies. As with other approaches in clinical psychology and psychiatry, the apparent clinical utility and face validity of such techniques seem to outweigh scientific reservations concerning their external validity.

Another distinguishable set of treatment studies involves the enhancement and improvement of behavioral and attitudinal compliance and subsequent physical control of disease. Behavioral researchers have become quite interested in analyzing the specific tasks of various medical regimens associated with various chronic diseases so as to gear therapeutic techniques toward improving the child's and parents' abilities to successfully complete these tasks. Within this approach it could be argued that a *disease-specific* model of assessment and treatment is clearly more relevant in practice as compared with globalized models of chronic illness. Consider the extensive work in diabetes mellitus, a disease which requires regular and frequent metabolic monitioring, daily insulin injections, close attention to lifestyle factors such as diet and exercise, and fairly frequent visits to health care facilities to assess disease control. Several excellent and clinically useful reviews of treatment outcome studies with diabetes and other chronic illnesses are available elsewhere (Delamater, 1985; Johnson, 1980, 1988; Masek, Fentress & Spirito, 1984).

Operant-behavioral techniques have been most commonly applied to regimen adherence problems within diabetes, asthma, and generalized chronic pain syndromes such as migraine headache and recurrent abdominal pain. As noted previously, these approaches have emphasized improvement of the child's adherence to the medical regimen. In the case of diabetes mellitus this would include shaping the child's behavior toward increased attention to diet, regularity of exercise, adequacy of metabolic monitoring and insulin administration, frequent scheduling of medical checkups and attendance at necessary office visits, and accrual of knowledge regarding disease features, its requirements, and limitations. In the case of pediatric asthma it might include improving the child's and family's abilities to detect symptoms that augur the onset of a wheezing episode, and ensuring that prophylactic measures are taken (e.g., peak-flow levels ascertained, medications given, avoidance of allergenic materials). Again, the techniques found within this approach have been primarily behavioral in orientation, using an S-R paradigm and a functional analysis of behavior as the starting point for assessment and treatment. These approaches have clearly documented a rather impressive degree of efficacy (Melamed & Johnson, 1981).

A related group of studies has focused on the amelioration of pain, discomfort, and acute anxiety levels specifically related to disease symptomatology and attendant medical procedures. Again, behavioral techniques have been reported to relieve more stressful pain and anxiety reactions associated with various diseases and their treatment. Intractable, acute, or chronic pain, excessive anxiety levels prior to and during stressful medical procedures, and the dulling of perceptual sensorium have been targeted within this approach. Examples include studies of head, abdomen and generalized body pain alleviation through biofeedback (Masek et al., 1984), reduction of anxiety-related wheezing episodes in chronic asthma and cystic fibrosis through relaxation training (Creer, 1987; Schwachman, Kowalski & Khaw, 1977), and preparation for chemotherapy or stressful medical procedures via an array of behavior therapy techniques (Varni, 1981; Redd, Anderson & Minagawa, 1982). Basic reinforcement methods have also been applied widely in clinical cases where child motivation and behavior associated with stressful or painful procedures are of concern. And, some research, as well as clinical experience, combine to suggest that interventions work best when an array of methods are available which can be tailored to the child and the presenting problem.

We should reiterate that two major foci within the intervention literature appear to have yielded more clinically applicable findings as compared with competing treatment strategies. First of all, the child behavioral medicine approaches have shown broad application and effectiveness across various chronic illness groups, but these methods have been most prevalent and well developed in the diabetes, cancer, and pediatric pain literatures. Behavioral techniques such as biofeedback, relaxation therapy, and operant-conditioning procedures have clearly proven their relevance and effectiveness in the treatment of psychological and physical complications of chronic disease and subsequent outcomes. It is, therefore, somewhat surprising to see the relatively slow rate at which these valuable approaches are being integrated into standard medical thinking and practice around the country. Also, the behavioral medicine techniques used in the literature on illness and stress management have been found to have special applicability for specific target symptoms or behavioral goals, a trend that moves in the direction of desirable treatment-by-diagnosis type sensitivity.

From another vantage point, we would view the work on family processes and their derivative intervention treatment approaches as offering relatively sophisticated conceptual frameworks for more psychodynamic attempts to assess and treat the psychosocial problems of the chronically ill child. This is due, in part, to a longer and more pervasive attention to family factors in the clinical research literature and the consensus that the family provides the primary context for both the occurrence of adjustment problems and eventual change. For example, the emerging trend in family research that seeks to link various dimensions of family life, or coping style, to the specific demands and tasks of different disease types is a step in the right direction (Cerreto & Travis, 1984; Drotar, Crawford & Bush, 1984; Johnson, 1988). Also, attention to the role of parent-child conflicts and the social modeling of coping behavior within family systems have yielded clinically useful findings and techniques.

It is likely that broader theoretical and clinical models of family functioning and treatment will continue to be applied to the chronically ill in ways which will greatly improve our capacity to understand and intervene. Kazak (1989) has pointed out the appropriateness and potential value of a *family systems* approach to clinical work with the chronically ill child and family. She has also suggested that the *social-ecological* framework provided by Bronfenbrenner (1979) and others may hold special relevance to the chronically ill.

Approaches that have emphasized individual personality or behavioral characteristics, patterns of cognitive style and disease appraisal, and the role of self-psychological processes in the treatment of chronic illness or conditions have generally been less specific or operationalizable both in terms of the methods used and in the measurement of clinical outcomes. Again, it is possible that the largely theoretical nature of these approaches does not allow them to be readily tested via empirical research techniques. It is clear from the existing research literature and clinical experience, however, that these factors are important and will be essential to our applied work with chronically ill children.

CASE STUDIES

We began this book with several illustrative case studies to introduce the reader to many of the complex issues which often characterize childhood chronic illness. At this point, we would like to return to the case-study approach to highlight some broader issues relevant to clinical intervention.

Jimmy

Jimmy was a 6-year-old child who was brought to a community mental health clinic with the presenting problem of inordinate fears associated with monsters, the dark, new places, strangers, and thunderstorms. He was also reported to have been diagnosed with moderately serious asthma, which first appeared during infancy and had been treated with several drugs that failed to keep his condition in adequate control consistently. He had been hospitalized over 10 times during the preceeding 5-year period for acute asthmatic attacks and had numerous visits to the family doctor and allergist. Currently, the child was reported to evidence wildly excitable behavior at the mere mention of any feared stimuli, or in response to any self-induced thoughts about them. A movie or conversation could provoke these fears and the family would be caught up in his panicky behaviors for lengthy periods of time thereafter. They would attempt to calm him down by talking to him, holding him, and so on. During these episodes he would also behave in a manner that seemed immature, irrational, and even bizarre to the parents, such as hiding under his bed or in the closets, crying inconsolably, or running through the house in a highly anxious state. At these times he would begin to hyperventilate and the parents feared an asthmatic attack would be imminent although this had not yet occurred. At other times, however, the child was described as rather pleasant and eager-to-please and presented few management difficulties for the parents and seemed to be more mature than his years would suggest. His excessive fearfulness had been noticed prior to the age of five but seemed to become appreciably worse soon thereafter.

The parents themselves were able to make useful connections between another source of panic in the family, namely Jimmy's sudden and acute asthma attacks, and the quality of the child's relatively new fears, as well as their own response to each. The parents had sought advice from their pediatrician who counseled them that most children had fears of this kind but did not necessarily display behaviors this unusual or pronounced. They were urged to seek the opinion of a child psychiatrist in the area. After meeting with the family for several sessions the psychiatrist recommended a psychological assessment of the child with an orientation toward a behavioral approach to the reduction of the irrational fears and parent counseling around the problems with the child's physical disease and unusual behaviors. The psychiatrist advised that if this approach was not successful then psychopharmacologic interventions might need be considered.

Sessions with the child primarily focused on initiating *systematic desensitization* procedures combined with teaching the child simple relaxation strategies that could be used in the face of fear-generating objects, ideation, or situations. This therapeutic approach was used for about 10 sessions with moderate success. The child's intensity and frequency of phobic behavior was reduced, but not eradicated. Subsequent sessions with the parents revealed that their own comparisons between their preparations for, and reactions to, Jimmy's acute asthma episodes might be practically useful. Choosing to set aside excessive speculation about the actual relations between the two phenomena, the therapist, in this case, elected to explore whether or not the parents and child might successfully cope with both problem situations using similar behavioral and cognitive strategies of response.

Clinical Issues. Again we can detect the possibility of a normal and expectable developmental pattern colliding with a familial dynamic that has been induced by reaction to a chronic illness. The rather common clinical pattern of management-by-crisis in moderate to severe cases of pediatric asthma, that was also characteristic of Jimmy's situation, had striking comparisons with his own reactions to the irrational fears of the early childhood period. Some might argue that such an inordinate response to phobic objects, as in this case, represents a more serious underlying pathology. Jimmy's treatment suggested otherwise in that increased personal control over his own excitability and emotionality, combined with improved adult role models, led to a considerable decrease in his phobic behavior and an enhancement of the parents' ability to deal with asthma-related crises. The primary-care pediatrician, after consultation with the child psychiatrist, met with the parents and specified a protocol for them in writing to help guide their decisions about use of medications, when to call the doctor, and under what circumstances they should go to the hospital. This counseling approach with the parents, and greater attention to their warranted and unwarranted fears related to Jimmy's asthma attacks, left them feeling more in control of the situation and prepared to think and behave proactively. Also, they claimed that this approach had assured them that their pediatrician could make time for some of their emotional concerns related to Jimmy's condition. Finally, Jimmy was taught to use a peak-flow meter which allowed him to self-monitor his actual expiratory flow rate, giving him an additional measure of personal control in the maintenance of his own physical condition. In this particular case a relatively noninvasive and multipronged clinical approach seemed best suited to the problem, prior to implementation of more in-depth psychodynamic therapies or uncertain psychopharmacologic interventions.

Kim

Kim was a 14-year-old boy with *sickle-cell anemia*, diagnosed at three years of age, who was now living in a single-parent family that was receiving public financial assistance. The range of stressors and chronic difficulties in the immediate and extended family were numerous. The presenting problem to the consulting child psychiatrist, however, was described in rather specific terms. The child was suspected of feigning illness and pain during hospitalization and perhaps, it was hypothesized, these symptoms represented an attempt to avoid discharge to home. His attending physicians were confused and uncertain how to proceed with this young man who claimed to have constant physical weakness, to experience excruciating pains in a variety of body sites, but whose general level of physical functioning appeared largely influenced by his immediate contextual situation. For example, when attending physicians made rounds in the morning or later in the afternoon he would be in bed, moaning and in apparent pain, and not ready to be sent home as planned. During the hours of the day and evening when the hospital playroom was open to the children he seemed completely recovered, or at least putting up an extremely good front, since he was actively and happily engaged in play with other patients. His mother reported that he had also missed a good deal of school during the past three years due to pains that appeared in the early morning hours but inexplicably seemed to improve dramatically by mid-day. Mother was tempted to interpret these pains, on occasion, as base manipulation, but felt unable to differentiate between real and feigned pain and was often left not knowing what to do. Kim's physicians admitted it was quite likely that Kim was experiencing occasional or even frequent pain associated with his disease. They also acknowledged it might be difficult to distinguish periods of genuine pain from exaggerated reports by the child. The psychiatrist was asked to help pave the way for a successful discharge of the patient, and to provide any clarification that was possible since the child would most certainly return to the hospital for future treatments.

Clinical Issues. Chronic disease, by virtue of its eventually leading to some level of differential treatment of the affected child, creates opportunities for major changes in a family system, in the child's emerging self-perceptions and identity, and in the functional role the illness and its symptoms will practically play in the normal everyday drama of growing up. Kim had learned to use his illness, and the obscurity his subjective reports of pain created in his well-intentioned mother and his physicians alike, to either avoid undesired situations (e.g., school) or to prolong desired activities, as in this case where he had come to prefer his stays in the hospital over the home. In this particular case Kim's preference was related to frequent adult attention, regular meals and snacks, limited schoolwork, and tangible amenities such as a color television in his semi-private room.

The difficulty and potential risk associated with separating out genuine pain versus manipulative and imagined pain can be considerable. Often the mental health practitioner is asked to perform such miracles, typically within a short period of time, and it is important to immediately recognize and declare the frequent impossibility of such efforts. The referral question about Kim, namely: *When was he faking and when was he telling the truth?* was the wrong question. Rather, the approach that led to better results was one which emphasized development of a rapport with Kim, followed by an evaluation of the desired goals of the child (e.g., avoiding discharge or school) and an exploration of alternate ways for him to approach the problem. Taking the weapon of illness symptomatology away from Kim through an examination of the underlying reasons why he might engage in manipulative behavior to avoid home or school was much more productive than elaborate attempts to confront him with partial evidence or to catch him in a lie. At times, clearly, such children are not communicative enough to allow such in-depth examination. This is probably true in a minority of cases, however, and establishment of a good rapport typically reduces this likelihood.

Another point that needs to be made here involves the importance of empowering medical providers such as physicians, nurses, and associated staff, with the ability to tackle problems such as those described in this case. The mental health professional who consults or treats such patients must realize the importance of putting much of the responsibility for desired change back on both the patient and medical health care providers who may eventually spend many more hours with the child and family than the psychological or psychiatric therapist. These hours are most often spent in the context of the medical care of the child, a setting which has traditionally been viewed as inappropriate for psychological exploration and/or support. We must continue to question the wisdom of such a view. This bias appears to derive from a system of medical education and service delivery that has not generally allowed the necessary clinical time or expertise to occur, and so these issues can be left to worsen until they reach a threshold that allows a psychopathological interpretation to be made.

In Kim's case a consultation would not have been necessary if more sensitive attempts to discuss his life at home and in the hospital were made, and if rapport were developed around his more personal issues, such as school performance and family milieu/relations. These issues are not the sole province of the mental health professionals and are exceedingly relevant to the comprehensive medical care of such children. A psychological understanding of Kim's issues might have precluded the necessity for his manipulative behavior and the arrival of the mental health expert.

Eileen

Eileen was a 16-year-old girl with *insulin-dependent diabetes mellitus* diagnosed two years prior to her referral to a mental health clinic for oppositional behavior and specifically for serious noncompliance related to her medical regimen. Her primary physician had attempted to allow the child to adjust to her disease during the preceding years while monitoring her physical condition closely through regular visits. These medical check-ups were often characterized by the child apparently portraying her compliance as quite good, reporting that she regularly monitored her blood glucose levels, carefully administered insulin injections, and watched her diet. However, summary laboratory values indicated she was in a very poor state of metabolic control. Her mother corroborated this conclusion, reporting that the child both actively and passively resisted the medical regimen. Parents also reported that the child had always been one who "tested limits" and had been a behavior problem for them dating from the preschool period. She first got into serious trouble in school in the third grade and she was eventually counseled regularly by the school social worker in connection with behavioral outbursts in class. She had never been seen by a mental health professional outside of the school, however. With the onset of diabetes mellitus at 14 years of age, the mother perceived everything worsening beginning with her refusal to take seriously the threat of possible health consequences and a reduced life expectancy if she did not comply with the medical regimen prescribed by her physicians. It was felt by all involved that Eileen had an excellent understanding of the nature of her disease and the relationship between her condition and the somewhat complicated precautions she needed to use to maintain glycemic control. However, she had never displayed a sense of the seriousness of the situation and, thus, her attitude was judged to be quite poor.

Soon after diagnosis, the parents reported, Eileen would use her completion of various diabetes tasks to elicit or extort special favors or material objects from them. She would often refuse to take her insulin unless promised money or a desired object such as a record or an article of clothing. Father and mother claimed they foolishly submitted to this manipulation by the child thinking that it was just a matter of time until she would realize how important attention to the disease would be to the child herself. This had not occurred, however, and now the child was needing to visit the doctor often for symptoms related to *hypoglycemia* (a condition of low blood sugar manifested by increased thirst and a need for frequent urination). And, the child was reported to have had one incident of *ketoacidosis* (a condition of inordinately high blood sugar levels leading to nausea, vomiting, abdominal pain and even coma or death if left untreated) for which she had been hospitalized for a few days. That incident had led to a strong suggestion by medical staff that the parents seek some type of child or family counseling.

Clinical Issues. As we noted in Chapter 4, there is a recurrent suggestion in the clinical literature on the behavioral and/or psychiatric outcomes of chronic illness during childhood that those who develop more serious psychological problems after disease onset are more likely to have had a prior history of interactional and/or behavioral difficulties than those who do not. Prospective studies of this trend have been extremely difficult to perform since we cannot know in advance which children in the heterogeneous population will develop specific chronic illnesses. From a theoretical perspective, however, it has been suggested that a variety of individual and familial factors that exist before the onset of a chronic disease or condition clearly act as additional risk factors for more serious long-term outcomes (Rutter, 1980). This can range from diagnosable psychiatric disorders or conditions to more subtle, but important, individual differences in children, their parents and the families themselves. In this case we encounter a child and family with just such a history dating back to Eileen's early years. The child's manageability and oppositionality to parents are described retrospectively as constant problems in this family. Such a situation should alert us to pay close attention to the psychological and family factors related to poor adjustment *at diagnosis* or soon thereafter. In Eileen's case another judgment might have been made earlier on to provide some sort of intervention to improve the parents' abilities to manage their child, and to attend to Eileen's disruptive behavior at home and school. In this case a "wait-and-see approach" was, in retrospect, not at all sufficient, although in many other situations we might choose such a course.

Another point to be made in connection with this case example involves the need for identifying a treatment model for the child and parents that emphasizes both extrinsic motivation for completion of parental and physician requests and nurturance of an internalized source of intrinsic motivation within this young woman. Overreliance on a highly structured approach imposed on Eileen might not have been as effective as a treatment plan which sought to work with her directly, either through individual or family sessions, to explore the meaning of the disease and the conflicts with her family. It is only through this channel that we might hope to see more rapid development of Eileen's own sense of personal responsibility for self-care. A common problem in clinical practice is the older child's active or passive resistance to strictly behavioral interventions and this often needs to be anticipated within a treatment plan. Although rather straightforward behavioral treatments can be extremely useful when certain motivational and/or situational criteria are met, they will be much less effective in cases that require a multimodal treatment approach. In some especially difficult cases the therapeutic maneuvers must include attention to individual and interactional dynamics prior to initiation of behavioral techniques.

Cindy

Cindy was a 16-year-old girl hospitalized frequently over a period of two years for treatment of brain cancer. Immediately prior to her diagnosis she had been thought to be in excellent health but she had experienced a sudden onset of an array of physical symptoms including vomiting, excruciating headaches, dizziness, and recurrent double vision. This deterioration in her health led to a medical assessment which quickly yielded a suspicion of the presence of *neuroblastoma* (cancerous or malignant brain tumors), and subsequently a specific diagnosis of *primitive neural tumors* was made. Radiologic tests revealed two moderately sized tumors that showed evidence of *metastasis* (a spreading of malignant cells in the brain). Cindy was unresponsive to chemotherapy and subsequent radiation therapy resulted in only partial remission of her tumors. Her prognosis was poor and over a relatively brief time this young woman's physical appearance, psychoemotional status, and overall quality of life were greatly diminished. Lengthy and repeated hospitalizations, frequent bouts of vomiting and nausea associated with her disease and treatments, total hair loss, significant weight loss, and increasing familial upset predominantly characterized the final year of Cindy's relatively brief life.

A consultation with a pediatric social worker was requested when resident physicians and nurses complained that Cindy's mother and father were becoming increasingly difficult to work with. Staff complained that the parents did not seem to be generally accepting of their daughter's fate, choosing to hope unrealistically for a miracle. Emotionally, they fluctuated between periods of intense anger, sadness, anxiety, bewilderment, and even periods of cheerfulness during those times when Cindy seemed to be doing better. These fluctuations on the parents' part were viewed as interfering with the completion of essential medical tasks. Specifically, the parents were reportedly concerned about the necessity and rationale for various medical procedures and medicines, whereas previously they had been very compliant with the medical staff's wishes. The mother refused to leave Cindy's side much of the time despite the staff's judgment that her own emotional well-being was suffering. The situation had worsened recently with another treatment failure and relapse. There was also a clearly detectable pattern emerging in which staff sought to avoid frequent or unnecessary contact with both Cindy and her parents. At the point of consultation the child was judged to have a terminal and deteriorating medical condition and physicians were seeking authorization from the parents that would allow the child to die naturally rather than require elaborate methods to resuscitate her with little or no hope for improvement in her disease. It was felt, based on past experience with the parents, that they would meet this issue with considerable upset and active resistance or opposition. Also, there was an interpretation on the part of certain key medical staff that the family was actively denying the seriousness of the situation and that they should have "moved on to a stage of acceptance by now." Communication between the parents and the medical staff had become so poor by this time that a resolution did not seem possible without some form of outside intervention. The pediatric social worker was called in to work with the family.

Clinical Issues. The clinical problems that can arise around the death of a seriously ill child, in terms of the child herself, the family, and the medical providers are considerable. Many common themes are touched upon in this case example, including the question of what is an optimal coping or bereavement process, the intense strains in the patient-provider relationship that can occur as a life-threatening disease progresses and treatments fail, and the rather remarkable qualitative changes that can characterize the care of the chronically ill as they linger in the hospital or at home, gradually moving closer to death. Due to the improved mortality rates in the past 20 years in childhood and adolescent chronic diseases, and reductions in acute diseases (see Chapter 2), the complexion of inpatient pediatric care is now rapidly changing in this country toward greater emphasis on the care of chronically ill children across their lifespan. Thus, situations like Cindy's, although extreme and dire, serve to illustrate many of the clinical issues which will be encountered more and more in secondary and tertiary-level health settings.

Our expectations regarding the course of human coping with this type of dramatic life stress, be they derived from personal philosophies or our readings of theoretical work on death and dying, can often be value laden and quite inaccurate for the individual case. The formerly prevailing view of the grief process as one that conforms to a predictable series of cognitive and emotional stages now appears clinically simplistic. In fact, a wide range of coping responses has been observed during the grief and bereavement process which refutes a perspective that seeks to make specific predictions about the course of psychological adaptation. Also, the common pattern of psychological denial, often clinically viewed as a relatively primitive defense mechanism in traditional psychodynamic formulations, can be extremely effective as a psychological reaction to overwhelming life stress as in the case of this cancer victim and her family. The longer-term outcomes associated with patterns of denial are not well known, however.

Religiosity, or belief in a higher power and the potential for miracles, which is sometimes frowned upon by those who do not share such belief systems, also appears to be a useful and effective coping mechanism for the terminally ill and their families. When conflicting methods and expectations for dealing with stress collide and create tension and/or clinical problems, the most appropriate intervention model is one which emphasizes mediation and the development of a mutual respect between patients, their family members, and health care providers. This approach would attempt to allow each person involved with a difficult case, such as Cindy's, to dispense with blame or preconceived notions directed at patients and parents who, for whatever reason, cannot conform to staff expectations.

SUMMARY

Our overview of professional orientations in pediatric medicine, nursing, medical social work, child health psychology, and child psychiatry provided in this chapter, along with an overview of the range of clinical techniques and approaches reported in the literature, should combine to introduce the reader to a broad range of very complex and challenging issues, as well as some practical problems within this exciting and emerging field. As noted previously, the psychometric armamentarium and the general backdrop for the assessment, diagnosis and treatment of chronically ill children primarily derive from the broader child mental health field. However, increased interest in the needs and care of these children in pediatric medicine and child health psychology is beginning to reap valuable and innovative contributions, some of which we have reviewed or alluded to in this or previous chapters. As applications of these methods and concepts to physically ill children and their families increase, a body of knowledge will gradually evolve which may provide the foundation for a more distinct and specialized approach to the clinical problems and issues this group of children and families present. Currently, however, we generally lack a cohesive and well formulated model for clinical assessment and intervention with chronically ill children and their families.

6

FINAL COMMENTS

OBSTACLES TO PROGRESS

Many factors have combined to delay clinical and research interest in the development and psychological well-being of chronically ill or disabled children. First of all, these children present with physiological symptoms which can be long-term and often unrelenting. This fact can render traditional mental health therapies seemingly ineffective or inadequate, especially when the target is major psychological change or *cure*. Even Westernized medicine, with a traditional emphasis on effecting complete and dramatic cure, has been hard pressed to provide a model for the comprehensive medical care and treatment of the chronically ill. Within health care systems psychological support of these individuals has typically been provided by practitioners at various levels of the nursing or social work professions, the clergy, self-help support networks, and most commonly, by family members. By and large, organized services continue to be sorely lacking, as is a definitive policy relevant to how such services should be delivered.

A second factor that continues to delay clinical attention to the chronically ill in both medical and mental health service delivery systems is the pervasive difficulty associated with obtaining reimbursement for psychological, social, and essential supportive services to this population (Hobbs et al., 1985; Starfield, 1985). Consider the fact that the current DSM-III-R nosology seems to contain only a few categories relevant to the chronically ill child. Most notable among these being the *adjustment reactions*. However, moves in several states to limit or eradicate third-party reimbursement for this class of diagnosis is a bit unsettling. Health planners are just now beginning to assess the immense costs this patient population incurs or will incur in the future as their ultimate longevity is increased via medical technology. The next decade may continue to be oriented towards dramatic reductions in health care services and expenditures. Further cut-backs in reimbursement for mental health services, as well as support for preventitive efforts, such as patient education and counseling, could be the predominant pattern of the future.

A third obstacle has arisen from resistance by several generations of mental health providers who have not had specialized training with such patient populations or who have not seen such patients as appropriately served using the dominant theoretical and treatment approaches of the past 50 years, namely the psychoanalytic method and its ego-psychological or psychodynamic derivatives. With the advent of cognitive, developmental, behavioral, and familial/systemic models of mental health assessment and intervention we have witnessed a much greater willingness to adapt contemporary psychotherapeutic techniques to the needs of the medically ill child and her family. Conversely, pediatric professionals have not typically received adequate training to equip them to intervene psychologically with such children. Despite their good intentions, and rather unique positioning for preventive and interventive efforts, pediatricians and their existing health care practices have far to go in this area. Efforts to improve this state of affairs have been sparse and not well organized, and ongoing confusion about who is best equipped and/or situated to serve this population continues to slow progress. No single provider type appears to have all of the skills and resources to meet the multiple needs of the chronically ill child. Current expansion and redefinition in several key health care disciplines, however, promise to promote greater attention to chronic illness and other handicapping conditions in the future, and perhaps a greater consensus regarding the need for multidisciplinary service delivery systems and multimodal treatment approaches. Fiscal constraints in the health care industry, however, will probably continue to limit this process and the full range of possibilities.

The presumption that someone else will take care of the psychological and social problems of the chronically ill has also typified practice, research and funding patterns in this area. Some might argue that the field of chronic illness has been too broad to allow programmatic research efforts since many different types of illnesses would need to be included, and traditional medicine has already effectively compartmentalized diseases via an elaborate system of subspecialization.

To make matters even more complex, a meaningful demarcation between chronic illnesses and other handicapping conditions (e.g., blindness, mental retardation, and so on) is often not available, serving to again broaden the phenomena which lead to difficulties in attempts toward greater specialization when warranted. And finally, the question of who should be studying the phenomenon of chronic illness in childhood has not been fully resolved, thus slowing quantitative research and restricting its essential funding base. As in the clinical arena, a view has emerged in recent years that supports multidisciplinary research projects on adjustment to chronic disease. What we have witnessed during the past 20 years, however, has largely been sporadic empirical research on the subject, typically with a narrow focus on several specific illnesses that affect children, most notably polio, diabetes, cystic fibrosis, muscular dystrophy, and asthma. Research on less common diseases with onset in childhood or adolescence often consist of no more than one or two studies with relevance to psychosocial or developmental concerns. Qualitative and opinion-based articles and books have been much more available, largely within less empirically oriented journals and publications out of the mainstream of Western scientific medicine.

We should not fool ourselves into thinking that the circumstances of the chronically ill are currently at the fore of medical and policy research in the United States. Rather, this is only one of many items being placed on the health care planning agenda for the next century in this country. It has a growing number of advocates within various professional disciplines, however, and grassroots support from the families and friends of affected children. And, as the U.S. population ages we will inevitably see increased social and political emphasis on the care of the elderly and infirmed which will almost certainly derive direct and indirect benefits for the chronically ill child. It is somewhat ironic that this demographic trend may eventually serve as one of the more essential social catalysts in the development of more comprehensive services and a national policy for the chronically ill.

PROMISING DIRECTIONS FOR RESEARCH AND PRACTICE

We have noted that the quality and quantity of psychosocial research on chronically ill children and their families has been inadequate. Again, this fact coincides with the sociohistorical and professional issues mentioned previously. In addition, the reluctance on the part of mainstream, laboratory-based medical science to support social and behavioral research in this area has reduced funding possibilities within an already competitive arena (Hobbs et al., 1985). Studies of the psychosocial aspects of chronic illness must attempt to overcome preexisting biases against social science research, which can be found in traditional medicine, as well as a broad and pervasive lack of interest in examining chronic conditions.

Psychological treatment studies with chronically ill children must wage the larger battles among conflicting theoretical orientations which characterize our traditional mental health approaches, while at the same time attempting to demonstrate the efficacy of a particular therapeutic approach to this special population.

Aside from these broader problems, Drotar (1989) has provided a very useful description of the array of practical and logistical difficulties associated with research on chronically ill children. He brings our attention to the inherent problems which can characterize attempts to achieve cross-disciplinary collaboration, a seemingly essential ingredient in medical-psycholological research, and to the often burdensome tasks related to actual data collection in medically ill samples of children and the marshaling of institutional support for psychological research within health care settings.

We have pointed out the importance of a sensitivity to those features that are relevant across various disease types *as well as* aspects which can be associated more narrowly with specific childhood diseases. An example of one major disease-specific factor to be considered is the nature of medical treatments that are necessary to improve the child's functional status. Also, the predictability of the disease's natural course is a factor that can vary dramatically across chronic illnesses. Researchers in juvenile diabetes and the childhood cancers have already begun to move in this direction but this has not been true in other major or less prevalent disease categories.

Attempts to formulate a more specialized developmental theory to account for normal and chronically ill children's social, emotional, and cognitive responses to disease and life trauma will need to emphasize the interrelationships among these three psychological domains and their behavioral manifestation. Such connections will not be simple to make. Obviously, prospective longitudinal studies will be valuable in this regard and yet they have been in short supply within the research literature. Attention to the timing of disease onset and the presence of preexisting risk factors within such studies, across disease types, will most fully aid our theoretical attempts to explain and predict mental health outcomes. Also, stage theories, which have guided much of the developmental research to date, appear somewhat restrictive and even inadequate for explaining the considerable variation in psychological understanding and adjustment among children of purportedly similar developmental levels.

Studies that examine the role of brain-related and cognitive sequelae of chronic diseases are beginning to show interesting and even unexpected results. Consider the fascinating questions emerging from the juvenile diabetes literature (Ryan, 1988). With the development and validation of more sophisticated neuropsychological measures, and application of such measures to other chronic disease types, it is likely that this approach will yield clinically useful findings in the future. Similarly, empirical studies of cognitive-behavioral and psychophysiological models of stress reactance promise to enhance more fully our knowledge about coping with chronic illness in the child and adolescent. Greater understanding of the neurologic, endocrinologic, and immunologic sequelae of both physical disease and acute or chronic exposure to life stress will eventually lead to the multifactorial explanations we seek in accounting for those cases of poor psychological adjustment and reduced physical and functional status. We would predict that the stress-and-illness research will provide the basis for more theoretically illuminating and clinically relevant work in this area. Therefore, it is clear that the current trend toward the multidisciplinary approach, both in research and practice, should continue.

Studies of chronic illness and family functioning, including the possible effects on parental relations and sibling outcomes, must continue to seek clinically relevant insights concerning the interactional processes that may mediate eventual child adjustment. Cross-cultural and subcultural studies would be welcome in this regard. Clinically-based descriptive and treatment outcome studies that examine family processes in concert with personological and/or behavioral variables will be clinically applicable. Such psychological characteristics and/or familial dimensions need to be associated with good versus poor outcomes in terms of physical as well as psychiatric parameters since findings could vary even within the same disease entity (e.g., some variables relevant to compliance but not to control in diabetes, and so on).

We would especially like to see more emphasis on research within the primary care pediatric or family medicine settings, the most common sites of ongoing education and treatment of the chronically ill child or adolescent. Most research to date has been hospital-based and may not be fully representative. For example, much more needs to be known about what pediatricians actually do for their chronically ill patients. One provider's definition of "continuity of care" may differ substantially from another's. The role of the pediatrician in supportive counseling is probably interpreted and manifested in many ways, and approaches to patient education will vary tremendously, as well. We need more data on referral practices from primary care and eventual case disposition following referral.

More distancing of the pediatric psychology and child health psychiatry subfields from traditional mental health methods and models may help to spawn a new generation of researchers and practitioners who will be able to create innovative approaches for chronically ill children and their families. We have indicated that psychopathologic models are inadequate for explaining much of the observed phenomena in this subgroup of children, although it is likely that some overlap will be found between a comprehensive theory of developmental psychopathology and a model that explains psychological coping with chronic illness. The development of clinical measures keyed to general and specific aspects of chronic disease during childhood is a promising feature of the child health psychology movement. Pooling of data across clinical research sites will be necessary for aggregation of adequately sized groups to norm such measures, but this is an effort that seems well worthwhile. And, indeed, multisite collaborative data collection has been the very approach that medical investigation networks have used in examining the prevalence and treatment of the childhood cancers, and with excellent results.

A standard method for rating the impact of chronic illnesses and/or conditions is needed. Some approaches are already available (Hobbs, Perrin & Ireys, 1985; Starfield, 1985) but they have not been universally embraced. These approaches involve measurement of functional status in terms of everyday activities and the patient's own determination of quality of life, a psychologically derived assessment. It is important to note that medical epidemiologists and biostatisticians have long been grappling with such measurement issues in adults, although little trace of this tradition can be found in child oriented health research (Katz, 1987; Spitzer, 1987). Such a standard would help to release the grip on psychological nosology which the DSM system now employs. It may also introduce a new research and clinical vocabulary better suited to the phenomenon of chronic illness.

It is our hope that the growing knowledge base relevant to psychosocial aspects of childhood chronic illness will manage to affect critical health care decision making during the upcoming decades. If too little information is available, or is not made accessible to health care policy makers, then these decisions will continue to be made based primarily on biomedical and economic data. Despite the formidable obstacles to supportive and psychologically oriented services for the chronically ill child, increased research and a better understanding of the psychological impact of chronic disease can only serve to bolster our attempts to achieve optimal prevention and intervention programs for these children and their families. Without such basic knowledge these children will continue to be misperceived and misdiagnosed. Many children in need of services will continue to go undetected by existing health care and social systems leading to a deterioration in overall quality of life and psychological adjustment.

REFERENCES

Als, H. (1982). Toward a synactive theory of development: Promise for the assessment and support of infant individuality. *Infant Mental Health Journal, 3,* 229-243.

Anand, K.J.S., & Hickey, P.R. (1987). Pain and its effects in the human neonate and fetus. *The New England Journal of Medicine, 317,* 1321-1329.

Anderson, B.J., & Auslander, W.F. (1980). Research on diabetes management and the family: A critique. *Diabetes Care, 3,* 696-702.

Anderson, B., Miller, J., Auslander, W., & Santiago, J. (1981). Family characteristics of diabetic adolescents: Relationship to metabolic control. *Diabetes Care, 4,* 586-594.

Andrews, C.A., Sullivan, J.L., Brettler, D.B., Brewster, F.E., Forsberg, A.D., Scesney, S., & Levine, P.H. (1987). Isolation of human immunodeficiency virus from hemophiliacs. *Journal of Pediatrics, 111,* 672-677.

APA Task Force on AIDS. (1989). Pediatric AIDS and human immunodeficiency virus infection. Psycholological issues. *American Psychologist, 44,* 258-264.

Aries, P. (1962). *Centuries of childhood: A social history of family life.* New York: Random House.

Armstrong, D., Wirt, R.D., Nesbit, M.E., & Martinson, I.M. (1982). Multidimensional assessment of psychological problems in children with cancer. *Research in Nursing and Health, 5,* 205-211.

Badinter, E. (1981). *The myth of motherhood.* London: Souvenir Press

Bancalari, E., & Gerhardt, T. (1986). Bronchopulmonary dysplasia. *Pediatric Clinics of North America, 33*(1), 1-20.

Barbour, S.D. (1987). Acquired immunodeficiency syndrome of childhood. *Pediatric Clinics of North America, 34,* 247-268.

Barnett, C., Liederman, P.H., Grobstein, R., & Klaus, M.H. (1970). Neonatal separation: The maternal side of the interactional deprivation. *Pediatrics, 5,* 197-202.

Bedell, J.R., Giordani, B., Amour, J.L., Tavormina, J., & Boll, T. (1977). Life stress and the psychological and medical adjustment for chronically ill children. *Journal of Psychosomatic Research, 21,* 237-242.

Belman, A.L., Diamond, G., Dickson, D., Horoupian, D., Llena, J., Lantos, G., & Rubinstein, A. (1988). Pediatric acquired immunodeficiency syndrome. *American Journal of Diseases in Children, 142,* 29-35.

Belman, A.L., Ultmann, M.H., Horoupian, D., Novick, B., Spiro, A.J., Rubinstein, A., Kurtzberg, D., & Cone-Wesson, B. (1985). Neurological complications in infants and children with acquired immune deficiency syndrome. *Annals of Neurology, 18,* 560-566.

Bibace, R., & Walsh, M.E. (1980). Development of children's concepts of illness. *Pediatrics, 66,* 912-917.

Block, J., Jennings, P.H., Harvey, E., & Simpson, E. (1964). Interaction between allergic potential and psychopathology in childhood. *Psychosomatic Medicine, 26,* 307-320.

Blos, P. (1978). Children think about illness: Their concepts and beliefs. In E. Gellert (Ed.), *Psychosocial aspects of pediatric care*. New York: Grune & Stratton.

Blum, R. (1984). Compliance with therapeutic regimens among children and youths. In R. Blum (Ed.), *Chronic illness and disabilities in childhood and adolescence*. New York: Grune & Stratton.

Blumberg, B.D., Lewis, J.M., & Susman, E.J. (1984). Adolescence: A time of transition. In M.G. Eisenberg, L.C. Sutkin, & M.A. Jansen (Eds.), *Chronic illness and disability through the life span: Effects on self and family*. New York: Springer.

Boukydis, C.F.Z. (1985). Perception of infant crying as an interpersonal event. In B.M. Lester & C.F.Z. Boukydis (Eds.), *Infant crying: Theoretical and research perspectives*. New York: Plenum.

Brazelton, T.B. (1979). Behavioral competence of the newborn infant. *Seminars in Perinatology*, *3*, 35-44.

Brazelton, T.B., Nugent, J.K., & Lester B.M. (1987). Neonatal behavioral assessment scale. In J. Osofsky (Ed.), *Handbook of infant development* (2nd ed.). New York: John Wiley.

Breslau, N. (1985). Psychiatric disorder in children with physical disabilities. *Journal of the American Academy of Child Psychiatry*, *24*, 87-94.

Breslau, N., Weitzman, M., & Messenger, K. (1981). Psychologic functioning of siblings of disabled children. *Pediatrics*, *67*, 344-353.

Brewster, A.B. (1982). Chronically ill hospitalized children's concepts of their illness. *Pediatrics*, *69*, 355-362.

Bronfenbrenner, U. (1979). *The ecology of human development*. Cambridge, MA: Harvard University Press.

Brown, E.R. (1987). Bronchopulmonary dysplasia. In H.W. Taeusch & M.W. Yogman (Eds.), *Follow-up management of the high-risk infant*. Boston: Little, Brown.

Burbach, D.J., & Peterson, L. (1986). Children's concepts of physical illness: A review and critique of the cognitive-developmental literature. *Health Psychology*, *5*, 307-325.

Burr, C.K. (1985). Impact on the family of a chronically ill child. In N. Hobbs & J.M. Perrin (Eds.), *Issues in the care of children with chronic illness*. San Francisco: Jossey-Bass.

Cadman, D., Boyle, M., & Offord, D.R. (1988). The Ontario child health study: Social adjustment and mental health of siblings of children with chronic health problems. *Journal of Developmental and Behavioral Pediatrics*, *9*, 117-121.

Cadman, D., Boyle, M.H., Szatmari, P., & Offord, D.R. (1987). Chronic illness, disability, and mental and social well-being: Findings of the Ontario child health study. *Pediatrics*, *79*, 805-813.

Cadman, D., Boyle, M.H., & Offord, D.R. (1986). Chronic illnesses, medical conditions and limitations in Ontario children. *Canadian Medical Association Journal*, *9*, 117-121.

Caplan, G., Mason, E.A., & Kaplan, D.M. (1965). Four studies of crisis in parents of prematures. *Community Mental Health Journal*, *1*, 149-161.

Carandang, M.L.A., Folkins, C.H., Hines, P.A., & Steward, M.S. (1979). The role of cognitive level and sibling illness in children's conceptualizations of illness. *American Journal of Orthopsychiatry*, *49*, 474-481.

Carraccio, C.L., McCormick, M.C., & Weller, S.C. (1987). *The Journal of Pediatrics*, *110*, 982-987.

Cassileth, B.R., Lusk, E.J., Strouse, T.B., Miller, D.S., Brown, L.L., Cross, P.A., & Tenaglia, A.N. (1984). Psychosocial status in chronic illness: A comparative analysis of six diagnostic groups. *The New England Journal of Medicine*, *311*, 506-511.

Cerreto, M.C., & Travis, L.B. (1984). Implications of psychological and family factors in the treatment of diabetes. *Pediatric Clinics of North America*, *31*(3), 689-710.

Chase, H.P. & Jackson, G.G. (1981). Stress and sugar control in children with insulin-dependent diabetes mellitus. *Journal of Pediatrics*, *98*, 1011-1013.

Cohen, M. (1984). The society for behavorial pediatrics: A new portal in a rapidly moving boundary. *Pediatrics*, *73*, 791-802.

Collins, G.C. (1988, May 24). Prevalence of selected chronic conditions, United States, 1983-85. *NCHS Advancedata*, no. 155.

Copeland, D.R., Dowell, R.E., Fletcher, J.M., Sullivan, M.P., Jaffe, N., Cangir, A., Frankel, L.S., & Judd, B.W. (1988). Neuropsychological test performance of pediatric cancer patients at diagnosis and one year later. *Journal of Pediatric Psychology*, *13*, 183-196.

Costello, E. (1988). Primary care pediatrics and child psychopathology: A review of diagnostic, treatment and referral practices. *Pediatrics*, *78*, 1044-1051.

Coultas, D.B., & Samet, J.M. (1987). Epidemiology and natural history of childhood asthma. In D.G. Tinkelman, C.J. Falliens & C.K. Napitz (Eds.), *Childhood asthma: Pathophysiology and treatment*. New York: Marcel Dekker.

Creer, T.L. (1987). Psychological and neurophysiological aspects of childhood asthma. In D.G. Tinkelman, C.J. Falliers & C.K. Napitz (Eds.), *Childhood asthma: Pathophysiology and treatment*. New York: Marcel Dekker

Crocker, E. (1978). Play programs in pediatric settings. In E. Gellert (Ed.), *Psychosocial aspects of pediatric care*. New York: Grune & Stratton.

Czajkowski, D.R., & Koocher, G.P. (1986). Predicting medical compliance among adolescents with cystic fibrosis. *Health Psychology*, *5*, 297-305.

Czajkowski, D.R., & Koocher, G.P. (1987). Medical compliance and coping with cystic fibrosis. *Journal of Child Psychology and Psychiatry*, *28*, 311-319.

Daniels, D., Miller, J.J., Billings, A.G., & Moos, R.H. (1986). Psychosocial functioning of siblings of children with rheumatic disease. *Journal of Pediatrics*, *109*, 379-383.

Daniels, D., Moos, R.H., Billings, A.G., & Miller, J.J. (1987). Psychosocial risk and resistance factors among children with chronic illness, healthy siblings, and healthy controls. *Journal of Abnormal Child Psychology*, *15*, 295-308.

Delamater, A.M. (1985). Psychological aspects of diabetes mellitus in children. In A. Kazdin (Ed.), *Advances in clinical child psychology* (Vol. 9, pp. 333-375). New York: Plenum

Delamater, A.M., Bubb, J., Kurtz, S.M., Kuntze, J., Smith, J.A., White, N.H., & Santiago, J.V. (1988). Physiologic responses to acute psychological stress in adolescents with type I diabetes mellitus. *Journal of Pediatric Psychology*, *13*, 69-86.

Delamater, A.M., Kurtz, S.M., Bubb, J., White, N.H., & Santiago, J.V. (1987). Stress and coping in relation to metabolic control of adolescents with Type I diabetes. *Journal of Developmental and Behavioral Pediatrics*, *8*, 136-140.

de Mause, L. (1974). *The history of childhood*. New York: Psychohistory Press.

Desquin, B.W. (1986). Chronic illness in children. An educational program for a primary-care pediatric residency. *American Journal of Diseases in Children*, *140*, 1246-1249.

Drash, A. & Berlin, N. (1985). Juvenile diabetes. In N. Hobbs & J.M. Perrin (Eds.), *Issues in the care of children with chronic illness*. San Francisco: Jossey-Bass.

Drotar, D. (1989). Psychological research in pediatric settings: Lessons from the field. *Journal of Pediatric Psychology, 14*, 63-74.

Drotar, D., & Bush, M. (1985). Mental health issues and services. In N. Hobbs & J.M. Perrin (Eds.), *Issues in the care of children with chronic illness*. San Francisco: Jossey-Bass.

Drotar, D., & Crawford, P. (1986). Psychological adaptations of siblings of chronically ill children: Research and practice implications. *Journal of Developmental and Behavioral Pediatrics, 6*, 355-362.

Drotar, D., Doershuk, C.F., Stein, R.C., Boat, T.F., Boyer, W., & Matthews, L. (1981). Psychosocial functioning of children with cystic fibrosis. *Pediatrics, 67*, 338-343.

Epstein, L.G., Sharer, L.R., Joshi, V.V., Fojas, M.M., Koenigsberger, M.R., & Oleske, J.M. (1985). Progressive encephalopathy in children with acquired immune deficiency syndrome. *Annals of Neurology, 17*, 488-496.

Erikson, E.H. (1963). *Childhood and Society* (2nd ed.). New York: W.W. Norton.

Feinstein, A.D. (1983). Psychological interventions in the treatment of cancer. *Clinical Psychology Review, 3*, 1-14.

Fowler, M.G., Whitt, J.K., Lallinger, R.R., Nash, K.B., Atkinson, S.S., Wells, R.J., & McMillan, C. (1988). Neuropsychologic and academic functioning of children with sickle cell anemia. *Journal of Developmental and Behavioral Pediatrics, 9*, 213-220.

Freud, A. (1952). The role of bodily illness in the mental life of children. *Psychoanalytic Study of the Child, 7*, 69-81.

Fyler, D.C. (1985). Congenital heart disease. In N. Hobbs & J. M. Perrin (Eds.), *Issues in the care of children with chronic illness*. San Francisco: Jossey-Bass.

Gergen, P.J., Mullally, D.I. & Evans, R. (1988). National survey of prevalence of asthma among children in the United States 1976-1980. *Pediatrics, 81*, 1-7.

Gilgoff, I., & Dietrich, S.L. (1985). Neuromuscular diseases. In N. Hobbs & J.M. Perrin (Eds.), *Issues in the care of children with chronic illness*. San Francisco: Jossey-Bass.

Ginsburg, H., & Opper, S. (1969). *Piaget's theory of intellectual development*. Englewood Cliffs, NJ: Prentice-Hall.

Gochman, D.S. (1985). Family determinants of children's concepts of health and illness. In D.C. Turk & R.D. Kerns (Eds.), *Health, illness, and families: A life-span perspective*. New York: John Wiley.

Gortmaker, S.L. (1985). Demography of childhood chronic diseases. In N. Hobbs & J.H. Perrin (Eds.), *Issues in the care of children with chronic illness*. San Francisco: Jossey-Bass.

Gortmaker, S.L., & Sappenfield, W. (1984). Chronic childhood disorders: Prevalence and impact. *Pediatric Clinics of North America, 31*(1), 3-18.

Gottfried, A.W., Wallace-Lande, P., Sherman-Brown, S., King, J., Coen, C., & Hodgman, J.E. (1981). Physical and social environment of newborn infants in special care units. *Science, 214*, 673-675.

Gould, M.S., Wunsch-Hitsig, R., & Dohrenwend, B.P. (1980). The formulation of hypotheses about prevalence, treatment and prognostic signficance of psychiatric disorders in children in the United States. In B.P. Dohrenwend, B.S. Dohrenwend, M.S. Gould et al. (Eds.), *Mental illness in the United States: Epidemological estimates*. New York: Praeger.

Grant, I., Kyle, G.C., Teichman, A., & Mendeles, J. (1974). Recent life events and diabetes in adults. *Psychosomatic Medicine, 36*, 121-128.

Green, M. (1983). Coming of age in general pediatrics. *Pediatrics, 72*, 275-282.

Grunau, R.V.E., & Craig, K.D. (1987). Pain expression in neonates: Facial action and cry. *Pain, 28,* 395-410.

Haggerty, R. (1984). Foreword to symposium on chronic disease in children. *Pediatric Clinics of North America, 31,* 1-2.

Haggerty, R. Roghmann, K.J., & Pless, I.B. (1975). *Child health and the community.* New York: John Wiley.

Hamp, M. (1984). The diabetic teenager. In R. Blum (Ed.), *Chronic illness and disabilities in childhood and adolescence.* New York: Grune & Stratton.

Hardgrove, C. (1977). Emotional inoculation: The three R's of preparation. *Journal of Association for Care of Children in Hospitals, 5* (4).

Heukrodt, C., Powazek, M., Brown, W.S., Kennelly, D., Imbus, C., Robinson, H., & Schantz, S. (1988). Electrophysiological signs of neurocognitive deficits in long-term leukemia survivors. *Journal of Pediatric Psychology, 13,* 223-236.

Hilgartner, M., Aledort L., & Giardina, P.J. (1985). Thalassemia and hemophilia. In N. Hobbs and J.M. Perrin (Eds.), *Issues in the care of children with chronic illness.* San Francisco: Jossey-Bass.

Hobbs, N., Perrin, J.M., & Ireys, H.T. (1985). *Chronically ill children and their families.* San Francisco: Jossey-Bass.

Horner, M.M., Rawlins, P., & Giles, K. (1987). How parents of children with chronic conditions perceive their own needs. *Maternal and Child Nursing, 12,* 40-43.

Hunsberger, M., Love, B., & Byrne, C. (1984). A review of current approaches used to help children and parents cope with health care procedures. *Maternal Child Nursing Journal, 13,* 145-165.

Hymovich, D.P. (1974). A framework for measuring outcomes of interaction with the chronically ill child and his family. In G.D. Grave and I.B. Pless (Eds.), *Chronic childhood illness: Assessment of outcome.* DHEW Publication No. (NIH) 76-877.

Izard, C.E., Hembree, E.A., Dougherty, L.M., & Spizzirri, C.L. (1983). Changes in facial expressions of 2- to 19-month old infants following acute pain. *Developmental Psychology, 19,* 418-426.

Jacobson, A., Hauser, S., Wolfsdorf, J.I., Houlihan, J., Mullen, J.E., Herskowitz, R.D., Wertlieb, D., & Watt, E, (1987). Psychologic predictors of compliance in children with recent onset of diabetes mellitus. *Journal of Pediatrics, 110,* 805-811.

Jamison, R.N., Lewis, S., & Burish, T.G. (1986). Psychological impact of cancer on adolescents: Self-image, locus of control, perception of illness and knowledge of cancer. *Journal of Chronic Disease, 39,* 609-617.

Jay, S.M., & Wright, L., (1985). Training psychologists to work with chronically ill children. In N. Hobbs & J.M. Perrin (Eds.), *Issues in the care of children with chronic illness.* San Francisco: Jossey-Bass.

Jellinek, M.S. (1982). The present status of psychiatry in pediatrics. *New England Journal of Medicine, 306,* 1227-1229.

Jessop, D.J., Riessman, C.K., & Stein, R.E.K. (1988). Chronic childhood illness and maternal mental health. *Journal of Developmental and Behavorial Pediatrics, 9,* 147-156.

Jessop, D.J., & Stein, R.E.K. (1985). Uncertainty and its reaction to the psychological and social correlates of chronic illness in children. *Social Science Medicine, 20,* 993-999.

Johnson, J.H. (1986). *Life events as stressors in childhood and adolescence.* Beverly Hills, CA: Sage.

Johnson, S.B. (1980). Psychological factors in juvenile diabetes: A review. *Journal of Behavioral Medicine, 3,* 95-116.

Johnson, S.B. (1984). Knowledge, attitudes, and behavior: Correlates of health in childhood diabetes. *Clinical Psychology Review, 4,* 503-524.

Johnson, S.B. (1985). The family and the child with chronic illness. In D.C. Turk & R.D. Kerns (Eds.), *Health, illness, and families: A life span perspective.* New York: John Wiley.

Johnson, S.B. (1988). Diabetes mellitus in childhood. In D.K. Routh (Ed.), *Handbook of pediatric psychology.* New York: Guilford.

Kaplan, S.L., Busner, J., Weinhold, C., & Lenon, P. (1987). Depressive symptoms in children and adolesents with cancer: A longitudinal study. *Journal of the American Academy of Child and Adolesent Psychiatry, 26,* 782-787.

Kashani, J.H., Barbero, G.J., & Bolander, F.D. (1981). Depression in hospitalized pediatric patients. *Journal of the American Academy of Child Psychiatry, 20,* 123-134.

Katz, S. (1987). The science of quality of life. *Journal of Chronic Diseases, 40,* 459-463.

Kazak, A.E. (1989). Families of chronically ill children: A systems and social-ecological model of adaptation and change. *Journal of Consulting and Clinical Psychology, 57,* 25-30.

Kellerman, J., Zeltzer, L., Ellenberg, L., Dash, J., & Rigler, D. (1980). Psychological effects of illness in adolescence. I. Anxiety, self-esteem, and perception of control. *The Journal of Pediatrics, 9,* 126-131.

Khampalikit, S. (1983). The interrelationships between the asthmatic child's dependency behavior, his perception of his illness, and his mother's perception of his illness. [Monograph 13]. *Maternal Child Nursing Journal, 12,* (4).

Kinsman, R.A., O'Banion, K., Resnikoff, P., Luparello, T.J., & Spector, S.L. (1973). Subjective symptoms of acute asthma within a heterogeneous sample of asthmatics. *Journal of Allergy and Clinical Immunology, 52,* 284.

Kohrman, A.F., Netzloff, M.L., & Weil, W.B. (1987). Diabetes mellitus. In A. Rudolph (Ed.), *Pediatrics.* Philadelphia, PA: Appleton-Lange.

Koocher, G.P. (1984). Terminal care and survivorship in pediatric chronic illness. *Clinical Psychology Review, 4,* 571-583.

Koocher, G.P., & O'Malley, J.E. (1981). *The Damocles syndrome: Psychological consequences of surviving childhood cancer.* New York: McGraw-Hill.

Korsch, B.M., & Fine, R. (1985). Chronic kidney diseases. In N. Hobbs & J.M. Perrin (Eds.), *Issues in the care of children with chronic illness.* San Francisco: Jossey-Bass.

Kotelchuck, M.C., & Wise, P.H. (1987). Epidemiology of prematurity and goals for prevention. In H.W. Taeusch & M.W. Yogman (Eds.), *Follow-up management of the high-risk infant.* Boston: Little, Brown.

Lavigne, J.V., & Ryan, M. (1979). Psychologic adjustment of siblings of children with chronic illness. *Pediatrics, 63,* 616-627.

Lazarus, R.S., & Launier, R. (1978). Stress related transactions between person and environment. In L.A. Perrin & M. Lewis (Eds.), *Perspectives in interactional psychology.* New York: Plenum.

Leventhal, J.M. (1984). Psychosocial assessment of children with chronic physical disease. *Pediatric Clinics of North America, 31,* 71-86.

Levine, J.D., & Gordon, N.C. (1982). Pain in prelingual children and its evaluation by pain-induced vocalization. *Pain, 14,* 85-93.

Lewandowski, L.A. (1984). Psychosocial aspects of pediatric critical care. In M.F. Hazinski (Ed.), *Nursing care of the critically ill child*. St. Louis: C.V. Mosby.

Lewiston, N.J. (1985). Cystic fibrosis. In N. Hobbs & J.M. Perrin (Eds.), *Issues in the care of children with chronic illness*. San Francisco: Jossey-Bass.

Litt, I.F., Cuskey, W.R., & Rosenberg, A. (1982). Role of self-esteem and autonomy in determining medication compliance among adolescents with juvenile rheumatoid arthritis. *Pediatrics, 69*, 15-17.

Macfarlane, A. (1986). *Marriage and love in England: Modes of reproduction 1800-1840*. Oxford: Basil Blackwell.

Matthews, L. & Drotar, D. (1984). Cystic fibrosis: A challenging long-term chronic disease. *Pediatric Clinics of North America, 31*(1), 133-152.

McAnarney, E.R. (1985). Social maturation: A challenge for handicapped and chronically ill adolescents. *Journal of Adolescent Health Care, 6*, 90-101.

McCracken, M.J. (1984). Cystic fibrosis in adolescence. In R. Blum (Ed.), *Chronic illness and disabilities in childhood and adolescence*. New York: Grune & Stratton.

McLaughlin, M.M. (1974). Survivors and surrogates: Children and parents from the ninth to the thirteenth centuries. In L. deMause (Ed.), *The history of childhood*. New York: Psychohistory Press.

Masek, B.J., Fentress, D.W., & Spirito, A. (1984). Behavioral treatment of symptoms of childhood illness. *Clinical Psychology Review, 4*, 561-570.

Mearig, J.S. (1985). Cognitive development of chronically ill children. In N. Hobbs & J.M. Perrin (Eds.), *Issues in the care of children with chronic illness*. San Francisco: Jossey-Bass.

Melamed, B.G., & Johnson, S.B. (1981). Chronic illness: asthma and juvenile diabetes. In E.J. Mash and L.G. Terdal (Eds.), *Behavioral assessment of childhood disorders*. New York: Guilford.

Melzack, R. (1975). The McGill Pain Questionnaire: Major properties and scoring methods. *Pain, 1*, 277-299.

Milos, M.E., & Reis, S. (1982). Effects of three play conditions on separation anxiety in young children. *Journal of Consulting and Clinical Psychology, 50*, 389.

Miller, L.P., & Miller, D.R. (1984). The pediatrician's role in caring for the child with cancer. *Pediatric Clinics of North America, 31*(1), 119-132.

Millstein, S.G., Adler, N.E., & Irwin, C.E. (1981). Conceptions of illness in young adolescents. *Pediatrics, 68*, 834-839.

Minde, K.K., Marton, P., Manning, D., & Hines, B. (1980). Some determinants of mother-infant interaction in the premature nursery. *Journal of the American Academy of Child Psychiatry, 19*, 1-21.

Minde, K., Whitelaw, A., Brown, L., & Fitzhardinge, P. (1983). Effect of neonatal complications in premature infants on early parent-infant interactions. *Developmental Medicine and Child Neurology, 25*, 763-777.

Minuchin, S., Rosman, B., & Baker, L. (1978). *Psychosomatic families*. Cambridge, MA: Harvard University Press.

Moffatt, M.E.K., & Pless, I.B. (1983). Locus of control in juvenile diabetic campers: Changes during camp, and relationship to camp staff assessments. *The Journal of Pediatrics, 103*, 146-150.

Moos, R.H. (1984). *Coping with physical illness*. New York: Plenum.

Moos, R.H., & Tsu, V.D. (1977). The crisis of physical illness: An overview. In R.H. Moos (Ed.), *Coping with physical illness*. New York: Plenum.

Mulhern, R.K., Crisco, J.J., & Kun, L.E. (1983). Neuropsychological sequelae of child-hood brain tumors: A review. *Journal of Clinical Child Psychology, 12*, 66-73.

Myers, G. (1984). Myelomeningocele: The medical aspects. *Pediatric Clinics of North America, 31*(1), 165-176.

Myers, G., & Millsap, M. (1985). Spina bifida. In N. Hobbs & J.M. Perrin (Eds.), *Issues in the care of children with chronic illness.* San Francisco; Jossey-Bass.

Nagy, M.H. (1951). Children's ideas on the origin of illness. *Health Education Journal, 9*, 6-12.

Nagy, M.H. (1953). The representation of germs by children. *Journal of Genetic Psychology, 83*, 227-240.

Natapoff, J.N. (1982). A developmental analysis of children's ideas of health. *Health Education Quarterly, 9*, 34-45.

Newacheck, P.W., Budetti, P.P., & Halfon, N. (1986). Trend in activity-limiting chronic conditions among children. *American Journal of Public Health, 76*, 178-184.

Newman, L.F. (1981). Social and sensory environment of low birth weight infants in a special care nursery: An anthropological investigation. *Journal of Nervous and Adrenal Disease, 169*, 448-455.

New York Times (1988, December 19). AIDS is reported as number 9 cause of death among children 1 to 14. p. 1.

Nickerson, B.G. (1985). Bronchopulmonary dysplasia. *Chest, 87*, 528-535.

Nolan, T., Desmond, K., Herlich, R., & Hardy, S. (1986). Knowledge of cystic fibrosis in patients and their parents. *Pediatrics, 77*, 229-235.

Nowicki, S., & Strickland, B.R. (1973). A locus of control scale for children. *Journal of Consulting Clinical Psychology, 40*, 148.

Offer, D., Ostrov, E., & Howard, K.I. (1984). Body image, self-perception, and chronic illness in adolescence. In R. Blum (Ed.), *Chronic illness and disabilities in childhood and adolescence.* New York: Grune & Stratton.

Olson, R.A., Huszti, H.C., Mason, P.J., & Seibert, J.M. (1989). Pediatric AIDS/HIV infection: An emerging challenge to pediatric psychology. *Journal of Pediatric Psychology, 14*, 1-21.

Orr, D.P., Weller, S.C., Satterwhite, B., & Pless, I.B. (1984). Psychosocial implications of chronic illness in adolescence. *The Journal of Pediatrics, 104*, 152-157.

Parcel, G.S., & Meyer, M.D. (1978). Development of an instrument to measure children's health locus of control. *Health Education Monographs 6*, 149-159.

Pendergrass, T.W., Chard, R.L., & Hartmann, J.R. (1985). Leukemia. In N. Hobbs & J.M. Perrin (Eds.), *Issues in the care of children with chronic illness.* San Francisco: Jossey-Bass.

Perrin, E.C., & Gerrity, P.S. (1981). There's a demon in your belly: Children's understanding of illness. *Pediatrics, 67*, 841-849.

Perrin, E.C., & Gerrity, P.S. (1984). Development of children with a chronic illness. *Pediatric Clinics of North America, 31* (1).

Perrin, E., & Perrin, J. (1983). Clinician's assessments of children's understanding of illness. *American Journal of Diseases of Children, 137*, 874-878.

Perrin, E.C. & Shapiro, E. (1985). Health locus of control beliefs of healthy children, children with a chronic physical illness, and their mothers. *Journal of Pediatrics, 107*, 627-633.

Perrin, J., & Ireys, H. (1984). The organization of services for chronically ill children and their families. *Pediatric Clinics of North America, 31*(1), 235-258.

Peterson, L., & Ridley-Johnson, R. (1980). Pediatric hospital response to survey on prehospital preparation for children. *Journal of Pediatric Psychology, 5*, 1-7.

Petrillo, M., & Sanger, S. (1972). *Emotional care of hospitalized children.* Philadelphia: Lippincott.

Piaget, J. (1952). *The origins of intelligence in children.* New York: International Universities Press.

Pinchbeck, I., & Hewitt, M. (1969). *Children in English society.* London: Routledge and Kegan Paul.

Pless, I.B. (1984). Clinical assessment: Physical and psychological functioning. *Pediatric Clinics of North America, 31*(1), 33-46.

Pless, I.B., & Pinkerton, P. (1975). *Chronic childhood disorders: Promoting patterns of adjustment.* London: Henry Kimpton.

Pless, I.B., & Roghmann, K.J. (1971). Chronic illness and its consequences: Observations based on three epidemiologic surveys. *Journal of Pediatrics, 79*, 351-359.

Pless, I.B., Roghmann, K., & Haggerty, R. (1972). Chronic illness, family functioning, and psychological adjustment: A model for the allocation of preventive mental health services. *International Journal of Epidemiology, 1*, 271-277.

Pless, I.B., & Satterwhite, B. (1973). A measure of family functioning and its application. *Social Science and Medicine, 7*, 613-621.

Pless, I.B., Satterwhite, B., VanVechten, D. (1978). Division, duplication and neglect: Patterns of care for children with chronic disorders. *Child Care and Health Delivery, 4*, 9-19.

Pless, I.B. & Zvagulis, I. (1988). The health of children with special needs. In *Research priorities in maternal and child health.* (DHHS Publication No. PHS3M 82-185). Washington, DC: Office for Maternal and Child Health.

Pollock, L. (1987). *A lasting relationship: Parents and children over three centuries.* Hanover: University of New Hampshire Press.

Pratt, C.B. (1985). Some aspects of childhood cancer epidemiology. *Pediatric Clinics of North America, 32*, 541-556.

Rae-Grant, Q. (1985). Psychological problems in the medically ill child. *Psychiatric Clinics of North America, 8*, (4).

Rait, D.S., Jacobsen, P.B., Lederberg, M.S., & Holland, J.C. (1988). Characteristics of psychiatric consultations in a pediatric cancer center. *American Journal of Psychiatry, 145*, 363-364.

Rashkis, S.R. (1965). Child's understanding of health. *A.M.A. Archives of General Psychiatry, 12*, 10-17.

Redd, W.H., Andersen, G.V., & Minagawa, K.Y. (1982). Control of anticipatory nausea in patients undergoing cancer chemotherapy. *Journal of Consulting and Clinical Psychology, 50*, 14-19.

Rivera, G., & Pui, C.H. (1987). Acute lymphoblastic leukemia. In A. Rudolph (Ed.), *Pediatrics.* Norwalk, CT: Appleton-Lange.

Roberts, M.C. (1986). The future of children's health care: What do we do? *Journal of Pediatric Psychology, 11*, 3-14.

Rodin, G.M. (1983). Psychosocial aspects of diabetes mellitus. *Canadian Journal of Psychiatry, 28*, 219-223.

Rovet, J.F., Ehrlich, R.M., & Hoppe, M. (1988). Specific intellectual deficits in children with early onset diabetes mellitus. *Child Development, 59*, 226-234.

Routh, D. (1988). *Handbook of pediatric psychology.* New York: Guilford.

Rudolph, A. (1987). *Pediatrics* (18th Edition). Norwalk, CT: Appleton-Lange.

Rutter, M. (1981). Stress, coping and development: Some issues and some questions. *Journal of Child Psychology and Psychiatry, 22,* 323-356.

Rutter, M., Graham, P. & Yule, W. (1970). *Neuropsychiatric study in childhood.* London: Lavenham Press.

Ryan, B., Connor, E., Minnefor, A., Desposito, F., & Oleske, J. (1987). Human immuno-deficiency virus infections in children. *Hematology/Oncology Clinics of North America.*

Ryan, C.M. (1988). Neurobehavioral complications of type-1 diabetes: Examination of possible risk factors. *Diabetes Care, 11,* 86-93.

Sabbeth, B.F., & Leventhal, J.M. (1984). Marital adjustment to chronic childhood illness: A critique of the literature. *Pediatrics, 73,* 762-768.

Sameroff, A.J. (1983). Developmental systems: Context and evolution. In W. Kessen (Ed.), *Mussen's handbook of child psychology* (Vol. I). New York: John Wiley.

Schowalter, J.E. (1977). Psychological reactions to physical illness and hospitalization in adolescence. *Journal of the American Academy of Child Psychiatry, 16,* 500-516

Seahill, M. (1969). Preparing children for procedures and operations. *Nursing Outline, 17,* 36-38.

Shapiro, J. (1983). Family reactions and coping strategies in response to the physically ill or handicapped child: A review. *Social Science Medicine, 17,* 913-931.

Siegal, M. (1988). Children's knowledge of contagion and contamination as causes of illness. *Child Development, 59,* 1353-1359.

Siegel, D.M. (1987). Adolescents and chronic illness. *Journal of the American Medical Association, 257,* 3396-3399.

Simeonsson R.J., Buckley, L., & Monson, L. (1979). Conception of illness causality in hospitalized children. *Journal of Pediatric Psychology, 4,* 77-84.

Simmons, R.J., Corey, M., Cowen, L., Keenan, N., Robertson, J., & Levison, H. (1985). Emotional adjustment of early adolescents with cystic fibrosis. *Psychosomatic Medicine, 47,* 111-122.

Smith, M.S., Gad, M.T., & O'Grady, L. (1983). Psychosocial functioning, life change, and clinical status in adolescents with cystic fibrosis. *Journal of Adolescent Health Care, 4,* 230-234.

Spinetta, J.J., & Maloney, L.J. (1978). The child with cancer: Patterns of communication and denial. *Journal of Consulting and Clinical Psychology, 46,* 1540-1541.

Spitz, R.A. (1946). Hospitalism: An inquiry into the genesis of psychiatric conditions in early childhood: A follow-up report. *Psychoanalytic Study of the Child, 2,* 313-342.

Spitzer, W. (1978). Quality of life and functional status as target variables for research. *Journal of Chronic Diseases, 40,* 465-471.

Stabler, B. (1988). Perspectives on chronic childhood illness. In B.G. Melamed, K.A. Matthews, D.K. Routh, B. Stabler, & N. Schneiderman (Eds.), *Child Health Psychology.* Hillsdale, NJ: Lawrence Erlbaum.

Starfield, B. (1985). The state of research on chronically ill children. In N. Hobbs & J.M. Perrin (Eds.), *Issues in the care of children with chronic illness.* San Francisco: Jossey-Bass.

Starfield, B., & Borkowf, S., (1969). Physician's recognition of complaints made by parents about their children's health. *Pediatrics, 43,* 168-174.

Stein, R.E.K., & Jessop, D.J. (1982). A noncategorical approach to chronic childhood illness. *Public Health Reports, 97,* 354-362.

Stein, R.E.K., & Jessop, D.J. (1984a). Does pediatric home care make a difference for children with chronic illness? Findings from the pediatric ambulatory care treatment study. *Pediatrics, 73*, 845-853.

Stein, R.E.K., & Jessop, D.J. (1984b). General issues in the care of children with chronic physical conditions. *Pediatric Clinics of North America, 31*(1), 189-198.

Stein, R.E.K., Jessop, D.J., & Reismann, C.K. (1983). Health care services received by children with chronic illness. *American Journal of the Diseases of Children, 137*, 225-230.

Steinhausen, H., Schindler, H., & Stephan, H. (1983). Correlates of psychopathology in sick children: An empirical approach. *Journal of the American Academy of Child Psychiatry, 22*, 559-564.

Stone, L. (1977). *The family, sex and marriage in England 1500 to 1800.* London: Weidenfield & Nicholson.

Trause, M.A., & Kramer, L.I. (1983). The effects of premature birth on parents and their relationship. *Developmental Medicine and Child Neurology, 25*, 459-465.

Trautman, P.D., Erickson, C., Shaffer, D., O'Connor, P.A., Sitarz, A., Correra, A., & Schonfeld, I.S. (1988). Predicting intellectual deficits in children with acute lymphoblastic leukemia. *Developmental and Behavioral Pediatrics, 9*, 122-128.

Tritt, S.G., & Esses, L.M. (1988). Psychosocial adaptation of siblings of children with chronic medical illnesses. *American Journal of Orthopsychiatry, 58*, 211-220.

Turk, D.C., & Kerns, R.D. (1985). The family in health and illness. In D.C. Turk & R.D. Kerns (Eds.), *Health, illness, and families: A life-span perspective.* New York: John Wiley.

Ultmann, M.H., Belman, A.L., Ruff, H.A., Novick, B.E., Cone-Wesson, B., Cohen, H.J., & Rubinstein, A. (1985). Developmental abnormalities in infants and children with acquired immune deficiency syndrome (AIDS) and AIDS-related complex. *Developmental Medicine and Child Neurology, 27*, 563-571.

Van Dongen-Melman, J.E.W.M., & Sanders-Woudstra, J.A.R. (1986). Psychosocial aspects of childhood cancer: A review of the literature. *Journal of Child Psychology and Psychiatry, 27*, 145-180.

Varni, J.W. (1981). Self regulation techniques in the management of chronic arthritic pain in hemophiliacs. *Behavior Therapy, 12*, 185-194.

Varni, J.W., & Jay, S.M. (1984). Biobehavioral factors in juvenile rheumatoid arthritis: Implications for research and practice. *Clinical Psychology Review, 4*, 543-560.

Vichinsky, E., & Lubin, B.H. (1987). Suggested guidelines for the treatment of children with sickle-cell anemia. *Hematology/Oncology Clinics of North America, 1*(3), 483-501.

Walker, L.S., & Greene, J.W. (1987). Negative life events, psychosocial resources, and psychophysiological symptoms in adolescents. *Journal of Clinical Child Psychology, 16*, 29-36.

Walker, D., Gortmaker, S., & Weitzman, M. (1981). *Chronic illness and psychosocial problems among children in Genesee County.* Boston: Harvard School of Public Health Publications.

Wallander, J.L., Varni, J.W., Babani, L., Banis, H.T., & Wilcox, K.T. (1988). Children with chronic physical disorders: Maternal reports of their psychological adjustment. *Journal of Pediatric Psychology, 13*, 197-212.

Waller, D.A., Chipman, J.J., Hardy, B.W., Hightower, M.S., North, A.J., Williams, S.B., & Babick, A.J. (1986). Measuring diabetes-specific family support and its relation to metabolic control: A preliminary report. *Journal of the American Academy of Child Psychiatry, 25*, 415-418.

Ward, J.W., Holmberg, S.D., Allen, J.R. (1988). Transmission of human immunodeficiency virus by blood transfusions screened negative for HIV antibody. *New England Journal of Medicine, 318*, 473-478.

Wasz-Hockert, O., Lind, J., Vuorenkoski, V., Partanen, T., & Valanne, E. (1968). *The infant cry.* London: Heinemann.

Wertlieb, D., Weigel, C., & Feldstein, M. (1987). Measuring children's coping. *American Journal of Orthopsychiatry, 57*, 548-560.

White, K., Kolman, M.L., Wexler, P., Polin, G., & Winter, R.J. (1984). Unstable diabetes and unstable families: A psychosocial evaluation of diabetic children with recurrent ketoacidosis. *Pediatrics, 73*, 749-755.

Whitt, J.K. (1984). Children's adaptation to chronic illness and handicapping conditions. In M.G. Eisenberg, L.C. Sutkin, & M.A. Jansen (Eds.), *Chronic illness and disability through the life span. Effects on self and family.* New York: Springer.

Whitt, J.K., Dykstra, W., & Taylor, C.A. (1979). Children's conceptions of illness and cognitive development. *Clinical Pediatrics 18*, 327-339.

Whitten, C.F., & Nishiura, E.N. (1985). Sickle cell anemia. In N. Hobbs & J.M. Perrin (Eds.), *Issues in the care of children with chronic illness: A source book on problems, services and policies.* San Francisco: Jossey-Bass.

Wolff, P.H. (1966). *The causes, controls, and organization of behavior in the neonate.* New York: International Universities Press.

Wu, R. (1965). Explaining treatments to young children. *American Journal of Nursing, 65*, 71-73.

Yamamoto, K. (1979). Children's ratings of the stressfulness of experiences. *Developmental Psychology, 15*, 581-582.

Yoos, L. (1987). Chronic childhood illnesses: Developmental issues. *Pediatric Nursing, 13*, 25-28.

Zeitlin, S. (1980). Assessing coping behavior. *American Journal of Orthopsychiatry, 50*, 139-144.

Zelizer, V.A. (1985). *Pricing the priceless child: The changing social value of children.* New York: Basic Books.

Zeltzer, L., Kellerman, J., Ellenberg, L., Dash, J., & Rigler, D.(1980). Psychological effects of illness in adolescence. II: Impact of illness in adolescents-crucial issues and coping styles. *Journal of Pediatrics, 97*, 132-138.

Zeltzer, L., LeBaron, S., Zeltzer, P. (1984). The adolescent with cancer. In R. Blum (Ed.), *Chronic illness and disabilities in childhood and adolescence.* New York: Grune & Stratton.

Zeskind, P.L., Sale, J., Maio, M.L., Huntington, L., & Weiseman, J.R. (1985). Adult perceptions of pain and hunger cries: a synchrony of arousal. *Child Development, 56*, 549-554.

SUBJECT INDEX

Acquired Immunodeficiency Syndrome
(AIDS), 21-22, 37, 50-51, 54-57,
92, 94-95
incidence, 55
psychological correlates, 56
activity limitations, *see* functional impairment
acute lymphoblastic leukemia (ALL), *see*
cancer
adaptation, 23, 36, 67-68, 76, 88-91
adherence,
see compliance
adolescence, 67-69, 74-75, 79-80, 90
compliance during, 68-69, 83-84
arthritis, *see* juvenile rheumatoid arthritis
asphyxia, 64
asthma, 39-41, 65, 77, 81, 87, 127-130
incidence, 40
medication side-effects, 41, 92, 95
psychological intervention in, 41,
125-126, 129-130
autonomy, 20, 46, 65-67, 69

Beck Depression Inventory, 98
bronchopulmonary dysplasia, 64

cancer, 32, 51-52, 69, 79, 80, 89-90, 94,
97-99, 124, 135-137
ALL, 13-16, 51-52, 95-96
incidence, 51
psychological sequelae, 52, 97-99, 113
treatment side-effects, 92, 95-96
cardiac disease, 43-44, 64, 80, 92
incidence, 43
psychological impact, 44
cerebral palsy, 88
Children's Depression Inventory, 98
Children's Health Locus of Control Scale,
81-82
Children's Locus of Control Scale, 82

chronic childhood illness,
and behavior problems, 19-20
and development, 24, 62-86
and mental health services, 32, 112,
138-140
and pediatric practice, 28-32, 66, 82,
110-111
and school functioning, 66-67, 92
historical trends, 9-10, 26-27, 110-114
incidence, 28-30
personality types, 87
compliance, 14, 19-21, 48, 62, 67-69, 74,
76, 80, 82-84, 125-126
concrete operational period, 73-75, 79, 81
contagion, 72
contamination, 73
coping, 12, 14-15, 17-18, 22, 24, 35-36,
80, 83, 90-91, 99-100, 121-123,
127, 137
see also stress
cystic fibrosis, 16-18, 32, 45-47, 78, 80,
83, 88-89, 92
and family functioning, 46
and self-image, 46, 68, 97
incidence, 45
physical manifestations, 16-17, 68
psychosocial correlates, 46, 68, 88

decalage, 74
denial, 16, 90, 100, 136
depression, 98, 99
developmental tasks, 62-69, 96
Erikson's stages, 65-66, 85
diabetes, 18-21, 32, 47-49, 66, 76, 78-84,
87, 89, 93, 97, 119-120, 125-126,
132-133
incidence, 47
metabolic control, 20, 47-49, 82-84,
93, 100-102, 105-106, 132-133
physical symptomatology, 19, 47

ABOUT THE AUTHORS

William T. Garrison is Director of Pediatric Psychology and Pediatric Research at the Baystate Medical Center in Springfield, Massachusetts. He is an Associate Professor of Pediatrics at the University of Massachusetts Medical School and is Visiting Associate Professor of Psychology at the University of Massachusetts at Amherst. He received a doctorate in Psychology at Cornell University and pursued postdoctoral specialty training in Clinical Child Psychology and Clinical Research at the Harvard Medical School and the McLean Hospital. He has been on the faculty of Harvard University, the Washington University in St. Louis, and was appointed to their affiliated pediatric hospitals. He is currently conducting a prospective, longitudinal study of very early onset diabetes mellitus.

Susan McQuiston is a Pediatric Psychologist at the Baystate Medical Center in Springfield, Massachusetts. She received a doctorate in Psychology at Purdue University and pursued postdoctoral experience at the Institute for the Study of Developmental Disabilities in Chicago. She was a Research Psychologist at the National Institute of Child Health and Human Development and was previously on the staff of the Medical College of Ohio/The Toledo Hospital Center for Women and Children. Her current research interests include family adaptation to the birth of a high-risk infant and the development of premature infants with bronchopulmonary dysplasia.